which CRAFT?

An Introduction to the Craft

RESEARCHED & WRIT BY SHAN

photography by Geoff King

COVER DESIGN & CALLIGRAPHY by Victoria Able

ILLUSTRATIONS by Terry Wick

House—of the Goddess™

33 Oldridge Rd London SW12 (01 673 6370)

First Printed 1986
Second Printing 1987
Third Printing 1988

House of the Goddess

ISBN No. 1 869973 00 3

Printed in Great Britain by
Whitstable Litho Printers Ltd.,
Whitstable, Kent

CONTENTS

Author's Note ....

WHAT IS A WITCH? 3
MAGICAL POWER..............................8
RITUAL 13
THE OLD RELIGIONS 17
THE REVIVED TRADITIONS 27
FAMILY TREE 31

INTRODUCTORY DICTIONARY 39

HOW TO BECOME A WITCH 62
THE GODDESS 66
THE GOD 72
THE CHARGE OF THE GODDESS 75
THE WHEEL 80

Booklist...
House of the Goddess ....

Acknowledgements...

FIRST & SECOND EDITIONS

TO THE GODDESS of course

TO BARBARA a mother among mothers

TO MIKE ARNOLD & QUENTIN who believed in me

TO ANNE & TO MARY who trained me

TO JO who brought me from scribbling to writing

TO ALAN who put me to work

TO SUE who provided the computer

TO VICTORIA who tamed it

TO TISSY & SAPPHY who helped a lot

TO ME who did it

THIRD EDITION

TO SUZANNE for many late nights

TO WALTER who came like a gift from the gods

There is increasing interest in Witches and what we do. Over several years of answering questions and teaching I have felt a need for an introductory book that would satisfy a basic curiosity without being an expensive item to buy. There are already several very good introductory books available (Valiente, Farrar, Starhawk and Gardner himself) but they cost too much for someone who is only in the initial interest stage. Also, initial interest does not want the wealth that these books hold, but something more in outline, with less detail, and yet still solidly informative. So here is my attempt to fill the gap.

It's a purification exercise as much as anything. Many of you who read it will probably feel pleased to have gained true knowledge about the Craft beyond the sensational stuff more often on offer. This will enable you to set it aside as 'interesting, but not for me.'

Craft Witches are a blessedly independent crowd, and constantly adapt their spirit with great vigour and creativity. So I have assuredly done less than justice to particular Witches and their ways, either because it is impossible to cover their variety in the scope I have here, or because of my own individual bias. Bias is a fact of nature in all of us, and I have tried to deal with it by allowing my own to be quite clear; you should not find it hard to make allowances where we hold different vision.

1987 edition

In the last year and a half WHICH CRAFT? has had a terrific welcome from its readers. As a matter of fact I never expected this little book to have such effect. I have been amazed and very touched that so many people say it meant a lot to them.

It shows that I'm a good writer, which is a matter of pleasure both to my readers, and to myself. But that alone would not require such an immediate reprint. What this shows is that there's a lot of people struggling to find deeper inspiration, a whole social movement towards an earth spirituality, of which this book is a small part.

1988 edition

Well, here's yet another edition of Which Craft? and much smartened up too. I'm really getting to enjoy publishing so there are more books on the way.

This edition is much expanded and matured - supposedly because I've matured! However most of the original is still here. It's been delightfully nostalgic going through my first book and bringing it up to date. Do write and tell me what you think.

Shan

Shan with her dearest friend & familiar.

What is a Witch?

There are three different ways of seeing a Witch:-

the stereotype;

the intuitive image;

and the tradition of Wicca.

The stereotype is an old hag dressed in black, who makes potions from nasty things, casts spells to control other people, and meets with her own strange kind to hold midnight orgies in the crypts of churches, or out in the wilds. There is a twisted truth in all this, although much of it is fantasy.
Witches are not necessarily old, for a start. They can be any age from teenagers to pensioners. Witches are both male and female. Many Witches study the use of herbs and other natural substances as aids to healing and mental work. Witches do cast spells, usually to strengthen the person the spell is for. Like any other working specialists they like to meet with their own sort from time to time, to have 'conferences' especially at the dates of the seasonal festivals. Witches are not in the habit of holding meetings in church crypts, and are no more likely to hold orgies than anyone else. Midnight is a favoured time for ritual, providing the babysitter will cooperate. Meeting in out of doors or wild places is desirable because it brings us closer to nature, but practicalities usually restrict rituals to someone's front room.

The intuitive image of a Witch appears when someone remarks 'She must be a Witch.' What they mean by it is that the person spoken of is unusually perceptive, perhaps odd or disturbing - eccentric - magnetic. In some way this person is felt to have a power, but not an obvious power which comes from physical strength, money, social position or public authority. It's a power hard to describe, and it merges into the world of wonders.
Recently some feminists have begun to use the image 'Witch' to mean a woman

who has connected to her own power, and to the harmony of nature. This is not a contradiction to the Wiccan tradition, but it stops short of the lengthy structured training usually undertaken by initiates of the tradition. It is closer to the intuitive image; a use of the power in the idea of 'Witch' as a kind of invocation.

The number of practising Witches in Britain today has been quoted at one million, but it is impossible to make any really accurate estimate. Witches know full well what kind of ignorant response they are likely to get if they are open about their faith, so they are discreet. You have definitely met and talked to Witches, but probably you did not know it. It is important to remember that Witches were horribly persecuted for centuries, and almost destroyed as a culture. Only in 1951 was the Witchcraft Act repealed to be replaced by the Fraudulent Mediums Act. It is no longer a criminal offence to be a practising Witch. However as many recent liberation movements have found, changes in the law are no more than a beginning. The public attitude about Witches is nervous and ignorant. To be known as a Witch can mean risking severe family disapproval, job insecurity, hostile neighbours, not to mention tedious rude jokes from new acquaintances! So Witches keep quiet, following a custom of discretion which enabled the Craft to survive the 'Burning Times'. A minority are now choosing to be more open, responding to an apparently more tolerant public interest. People seem a little less contaminated by christian thought police than formerly. But the many cases of injustice against minority groups indicate that the struggle for freedom of belief and lifestyle is far from won. We say thankfully that the 'Burning Times' are over - for now.

The tradition of Wicca has reclaimed, restored, patched and revived what was left after the christian persecutions. The Craft which has emerged from this reclamation project is an earth centred, self centred, life affirming tradition, with several growing branches. There are hereditary and traditionalist Witches, who are very private and seldom met. There are ceremonial Magicians, the secret agents of the occult. There are Gardnerians and Alexandrians, the sources of the renewed vigour since 1950. There are Celtics, Nordics and Seax, each with their own strain of inspiration from native culture. There are the Goddess saturated Dianics, and the feminist intuitive Witches. There is the vigorous Shamanic Craft. There are Pagans pure and simple who are not so formally trained or initiated but work in their own ways towards manifesting divinity, ecology and transformation. There are also poseurs, boasters, and self styled initiates grade ninety eight! In amongst all the various branches of the tradition, which are very different, it is tricky to generalize without immediately plunging into exceptions. Yet there is an essential core.

A WITCH IS A WOMAN OR A MAN WHO HAS TRAINED IN THE USE OF THEIR OWN NATURAL POWERS.

I'm afraid that's the best I can do as a potted definition, because of the aforesaid problem with exceptions to whatever I say. However the following are principles of our faith and life, so far as I know:

WITCHES...

★ **Witches** are spiritual. We understand that our human minds cannot hold the immensity of Wholeness for more than a moment's glimpse. So our teachings give us myth reality as a bridge to it. Goddess, God and Elements are our most frequent archetypes.

★ All **Witches** love and venerate the Goddess, as the creative origin of everything. She is the totality of everything that exists now, in the past, and in the future. She is the deepest Self within.

★ All **Witches** (except feminist Dianics) similarly venerate the God, the Horned One, Beloved of the Goddess. He is the Guardian and the Sacrifice, vigorous, sensual, gentle. Awesome and yet playful, he offers a striking alternative to the conventional idea of the masculine.

★ **Witches** are Green people. We all venerate Mother Earth, although how we express that varies. Many of us are active in Green politics and ecological work. Others quietly ensure that our use of outdoor places is done mannerly and tidily. Most Witches have a love of animals and plants.

★ **Witches** are drawn to natural cycles, to plants, animals, trees, groves, standing stones, stars, sun, moon, earth energy: Magic. We train ourselves to attune to and apply natural laws, and to understand them as far as that is possible. Unlike scientists we do not flinch from what is incomprehensible. If we can't understand why something works, we'll test it and use it anyway (for example, dowsing).

★ **Witches** affectionately call their religion the 'Craft'. The original Saxon meaning of 'craefte' was 'worth, integrity, skill, craft and power.' For Witches creativity is an essential part of our lives. Our personal crafts range widely; pottery, herbalism, woodwork, painting, dance, weaving, gem and metalwork ... as well as the Tarot, Palmistry, dream study, trancework, scrying, all forms of healing, and ritual. There again it is not only the older crafts that bring the inner to the outer, but also recent options like computers.

★ **Witches** hold the body in great respect, as the sacred gift of the Goddess. Witches are not ascetics. Their love of feasting, dancing, music, and joyous company may have given rise to the exaggerated orgy rumours in the hopeful fantasies of the puritanical. Where the body and all its capacities are held holy, then the maker of bodies, woman, is especially honoured. Women are the Goddess on earth. Sexuality is her essential energy, her vital current of life itself, her sacred call to union. 'All acts of love and pleasure are my rituals' she has told us, so Witches are usually freer of the poisons of guilt than most.

★ The **Goddess** is the original Trinity, Maiden, Mother and Crone. While the Maiden is still feted in modern consciousness so long as she's a good girl, the Mother has diminished to become a dutiful wife. Crones have been thoroughly suppressed, and replaced by little old ladies.

★ The five **Elements, AIR FIRE WATER EARTH & SPIRIT,** are the basics of our Shamanic philosophy. Wiccan ritual takes place in a cast circle, and calls in the powers of these Elements. The tradition teaches magical correspondences which follow deep seated patterns in our minds. So each Element has a cardinal direction (e.g. North) its personal powers, its hour of the day, season of the year, magical tool, plants, trees, totem animal, planets, jewels, colours etc. Similarities are easy to find between Craft, Tarot, Qabala, Freemasonry. All are part of a common Western esoteric tradition of philosophy.

★ **Witches** celebrate eight Festivals of the year, often called Sabbats.

SAMHAIN Oct 31 (Halloween)
YULE Dec 21 (Midwinter Solstice)
IMBOLC Feb 2 (Candlemas)
EOSTRA March 21 (Spring Equinox)
BELTAINE May 1 (May Day)
MIDSUMMER June 21 (Midsummer Solstice)
LAMMAS Aug 1 (Harvest)
KORE Sept 21 (Autumn Equinox).

6

These festivals are the spokes of the Wheel of the Year, marking the dramatic stages of sacred myth. The exact way the story is told varies a good deal from one branch of the Craft to another, but the core meaning is the same. Participating in a Festival brings us closer to the changes from one season to another, and to the moves of the soul on her journey through dark and light, pain and pleasure, in the cycle.

★ **Witches** heal. Many work in medical, hospital, therapy, social work or alternative medicine kinds of livelihoods. Whether or not our formal work is to do with healing, most of us develop healing skill if we do not already have it before becoming a Witch.

★ **Witches** practice divination, such as the Tarot, Astrology, Runes etc. We do so for deeper self knowledge, to help with key decisions, and to ask about future trends.

★ Most **Witches** believe in reincarnation. All understand the Web of Wyrd (karma).

★ For **Witches**, intuition is as highly respected as intellect. Where such oppositions as this arise in other faiths, Witches instead apply the fivefold Elements: knowledge, will, intuition, endurance and transformation, as aspects of the whole spirit. The duality of good/ evil, above/below, dark/light, superior/inferior, opens out into the star, the pentagram.

# Magical power

Would you like to attract money like a magnet? Is there someone whose love or sexual desire you'd dearly like to focus on you? Do you feel the need of extra strength to stand up to people and control events in your life? Do you feel in need of protection from psychic attack? Are you fascinated by telepathy, clairvoyance, astral projection, - with more than an occasional very private wonder if you might have such powers? Are you drawn to cosmic secrets? earth mysteries? arcane knowledge? revelation? hidden adepts of awesome wisdom?

Fear not, you're not alone. All of us if we're honest have felt some of these at some time in our lives. They are the reasons why occult books and correspondence courses sell as well as they do. Many a Witch's very first stirrings of magical hunger began like this.

What links these different feelings is a desire for power. Whether it is the fiercely pure power of knowledge, or the more practical power of influencing events, power is the name of the game. Most of us actually feel very little power in our lives. We are dominated by employers and working schedules, or the constant demands of children. We can be frustrated by lack of money, loneliness, or inner fears. Other people could provide what we want, but they won't. Sometimes the weeks and months seem to stretch ahead with endless boring tasks until through the empty hours dreams fade away. By contrast how exciting it must be to learn words of power, mystic symbols, ancient mysteries. We could learn to control people and events so that things go our way for a change. Or at the very least we can gain admission to an inner circle who are in the know. Then even though we still look ordinary, underneath we know we're special.

Examine the idea of power. Power means leaders, controlling people and things, being obeyed. Power belongs to governments, armies, the rich, the famous, scientists, the physically strong. Power means whirlwind, conflagration, torrent, earthquake. Power is obeyed, power is feared. Power is control. Most of our relationships are unequal, and we know well enough whether we are more powerful, or less so, in each of them.

Although being controlled, being less powerful, is not obviously desirable, in fact we often prefer it. Within the protection of someone stronger there are fewer decisions to make. Certain things are provided such as wages, law and order, regular companionship, a home. In return for these we undertake to some extent to obey, to be controlled.

Being powerful, on the other hand, brings more free time (perhaps), money, the support and admiration of others. But it also brings more decisions, anxiety, pressure to provide for others - and their contempt, even ganged up attack if they don't get taken care of as they expect.

However, most of us would still feel that we would like more power, not less. Well, magic does bring more power into our lives, but not the sort described so far. What we have examined so far is power as CONTROL, power over others, outer power.

MAGIC IS POWER FROM WITHIN, THE POWER OF CAPACITY.

Instead of getting what we want by making others provide it, whether these others are human or magical beings, magic inspires us and sustains us so we can provide for ourselves. Magic is about

IMAGES
IMAGINATION
WILL
CREATIVITY.

MAGIC IS THE ART AND SCIENCE OF CHANGING CONSCIOUSNESS ACCORDING TO THE WILL.

(Aleister Crowley, Dion Fortune)

9

A great many spells work by requiring you to repeat words and actions with a careful intensity, so that you are focusing more and more deeply on what you want, and its reality grows greater and greater. You start to believe in its possibility,
then its probability,
then its predictability,
and finally its inevitability.
You have created belief in your own power to make it happen, so then you do. If this were all (well, that's quite a lot really) magic could be parcelled up with faith, placebo effect and suggestion. But magic does not tell you to repeat mere random words and actions as its tools. They are selected and patterned instructions which fit the needs of very deep levels of the mind.
At shallower levels, where we do housework, factory and office work, we have changed radically compared to our ancestors. We make thousands of everyday adjustments to complex machinery that those ancient peoples would find bewildering. Of course we in our turn would find ourselves aghast to be dependent for survival on subtle distinctions between plants, roots, minerals, insects, animal noises and tracks, that are just part of the craft of the gatherer. But under the apparent differences between us and peoples of older types of society lie basic similarities. We feel secure with square shapes. We trust blue but we don't want to eat it. Enclosures, provided they're not too small, mean safety. Rhythms pounded steadily faster release us into excitement of mind as well as body. The seasons dominate our biochemistry. Colours, shapes, noises, smells, tastes, and emotional drives are the same as ever.
Magic uses these systems as language, the language of creation. Over thousands of years the original magical matrix has endured, only recently splitting into religion, science, philosophy, psychology, art, intuition, technology, divination, myth and the unexplained.

Magic directs the resources of the imagination through appropriate images, then energizes the will to reach down to deep places where we are all interconnected in a continuous reality. In the domain of the underworld we are not separate selves. Even in everyday reality the separations between us disappear under certain conditions. Deep down, connections may be made, or broken, which will only later appear in the outer world. Every event in the outer world has first happened within.

MAGIC IS WHAT TRANSFORMS IDEA INTO REALITY.

Before any action that you take there is an image in your mind of what you are going to do. The image may form only a fraction of a second before you act, it may be blurred and uncertain, but it must form for the brain to signal instructions to the body to act. This image is not 'real', not physical, and yet energized and manifested it becomes 'real.' The image of beans on toast in your head later becomes beans on toast you can eat.

Food is an especially appropriate example as it happens, for the Witch's cooking pot, or cauldron, is the central magical tool of transformation. What goes in it comes out changed, whether foodstuff, herbs for healing, or hopes and dreams.

The image is the crucial first step in any magical process, whether it's for making supper, or making a dream come true. Without a clear strong image of what I want I can hardly recognize the acts and tools toward it that come to my hand. Far too often we yearn blind, knowing we lack something but unable to remedy that because we are vague about what would satisfy us if only we had it. So first the image must be focused in the mind. A lot of magical training develops the ability to imagine through visualization work.

Next the image must be energized. If you are not completely honest with yourself about what you want, which is a common condition to us all, then your mind will divide against itself. The part that truly wants, will fight the part that thinks it should ... or is trying to be satisfied with less. A single undivided mind is necessary if you are to succeed. Apathy, lack of confidence, repeated unfinishings, mean you are in some way avoiding the nature of what you want. Magic uses various techniques for clearing and raising energy; breath work, chants, dances, moving meditation, music, laughter etc. But often we must face fear in order to proceed.

Fear is the immobiliser, the lurker in the depths. Fear is the place of lonely combat, pain, illusion, backtracking, uncertainty, the unexpected. In trials of anxiety and hurt we descend sometimes even to the break down of self, where bereft of all aid we hang in a state of obliteration, before we cycle upward again to renewed strength, and a different self. Magic teaches courage to face fear, intuitive insight to see through illusion, and always pleasure to sustain us against despair. As guides to the quest we have all the forms of divination; Tarot, palmistry, dream interpretation etc.

Divination is the art most frequently identified as magical. In truth it is not more magical than any other craft, but our society does not customarily prepare and train us to it, so it fascinates us. Divination provides some kind of tool for us to focus on, such as pictorial images on cards, a crystal ball, a candle flame etc. Meanwhile the intuitive mind is unlocked as the more conscious mind is kept occupied. The process is similar to providing interesting toys for a child so two adults can concentrate on their conversation. Practitioners such as Tarot readers, scryers, differ in how they describe their experience, but all describe some image of insight coming from beyond their everyday self. The equipment is not the real source of the reading, only its agent.

But divination does not rely completely on tools. Ordinary everyday events can give you powerful messages about how the great Web is weaving. If you keep making the same mistake, if you find the friends or lovers you have keep hurting you in the same way, if a coincidence keeps nagging, then the Web is talking to you.

People often come to me asking for help to make more money, or retrieve a lost lover. The deeper arts of magic are not about just rearranging reality like changing the furniture around. True magic is about accepting that outer events are signs for us to look within. Money, love, knowledge, tranquillity are abundant when we have made shifts within, and unlocked new power. They start to disappear when it's time for us to develop more wisdom and power. This is not a punishment because we've been lazy. It's just that when we're happy and comfortable we're not so flexible, we don't try new things. So if the Web needs to push us into new power, we may have to be pushed to desperation before we'll change. Once the change has been made, either money or lover returns as we wish, or we may find we are so different that what we want has changed too.

At last we come to the actuality of what we want. Often the active will is obstructed, so that we can learn more strength and wisdom. We wait, perhaps have to learn the magical art of doing nothing. Some would say this is the hardest of all. And then as the desired event comes to be we may find irony. It may have a hidden side we did not expect, and its completion brings with it new challenge along with the resolving of old ones. We must grapple with its practicalities and limitations.

Then finally we must let go, accept, and move on to another beginning.

12

RITUAL

The magical cycle through Air (thought) Fire (energy) Water (feeling) and Earth (acceptance) is the basis of Craft ritual. Ritual is essential to spiritual life, although how ritual is worked may appear very different in the various religious traditions. Some have lost sight of the original aim of ritual. The traditional phrases, gestures and display, remain but only as ceremony. Living ritual, by contrast, is less obsessed with word perfect litany, or exact etiquette, and more with an essential feeling of getting the job done. Not that an awareness of continuity with the past through following custom is not important; it is. But the first task of ritual is to enable its participants to undergo transformation (and I don't mean into bored observers). To live is to change. Change is interesting and stimulating, but also frightening and painful. We have within us parts that welcome change and move with it. We also have other parts that protect us and prevent us from being overwhelmed by changes, but these guardians can also resist, drag behind, cling to past states.

This applies to all kinds of passages of change: passing from summer to autumn, moving house, bringing a child into our lives, beginning a project or a job, falling in love, gaining money, losing money, surviving bereavement or separation, building oneself stronger, celebrating success, iilness, vows, making a friendship

any key process in our lives. Ritual underlines the event we are moving through, deepening it, so we live it with a richer awareness of its meaning. Ritual is a set of techniques, which over thousands of years, has been assembled by generations of practitioners into a fine art. Most modern religious rituals are performed by only one, or a few professionals, for a congregation of 'lay' people. Craft ritual is performed by every member, for themselves, and for each other. Every Witch is her/his own priest/ess. This is one of the reasons why an applicant for training as a Witch is frequently given an obstructive response to their first enthusiasm. The self reliance necessary to a Witch is such that many perfectly sincere people end up going elsewhere to find something less demanding. Craft practice is based on a good deal of solitary work. Only some Witches work in a coven, and even so, they still do a lot of their work alone. In a coven, every member is responsible for working a shared ritual. Priest + congregation is quite literally foreign to the Craft. The only limit on participation is the degree of knowledge each Witch has. Where less responsibility is put on newer Witches this is expected to change in due course with growth in knowledge and experience.

Craft rituals are structured so that certain stages are understood to work best before, or after, others. Briefly, ritual can be divided into seven steps. (However, this division into seven is no more than a convenience. The whole could be divided at different points, according to intuitive judgement.)

ONE PREPARATION As ritual is an opportunity to open out on deeper levels, which requires mutual trust and stability, so tradition wisely advises that all decisions should be taken as to how things are to be done before the ritual begins. As far as possible, no new work is suggested or initiated after this point. Once agreed, participants can trust themselves to the prepared sequence without wariness as to what is to come.

TWO PURIFICATION Next comes the need to set aside distractions and anxieties in order to give full attention to the task/s to be done.

THREE CASTING THE CIRCLE All Witches work in a circular space which must be carefully laid out and properly prepared. As any working space must be cleared and prepared so too must magical space. At this stage the Elements of Air, Fire, Water, Earth and Spirit are called to be present. This can be understood as both calling in an external force, and also that particular aspect of the self, to be fully present and active. Every part of the self is relevant in Craft philosophy; intelligence, will, emotions, body and spirit. None is less valued than another.

FOUR RAISING ENERGY Various ways can be chosen depending on the needs of those present, and the demands expected in the later stages. A selection of breathing exercises, chanting, dancing, music etc is used until everyone feels thoroughly energised.

FIVE DIRECTING THE ENERGY This could be said to be the heart of the matter. Needs for clarity, strength, guidance are attended to, and working tools consecrated. Spells are cast. Magical drama may be used, especially to express Festival mythos. Meditation and pathworking are employed and any form of divination practised.

SIX COMMUNION Having worked well we bring ourselves back to earth, with relaxation, and the simple pleasures of food, drink, shared thanksgiving, and laughter. Some more serious minded Witches prefer to keep the Communion until after the Circle is opened, so that this stage becomes the 7th and the next becomes the 6th. The nature of each is essentially the same though. Of course the ancient rite of Communion has been adopted by many later forms of religion, but has often lost its earthy, happy nature.

SEVEN OPENING THE CIRCLE Each Element in turn is bid farewell, in a reversal of the Casting process. The Circle is dissolved until it is needed again.

Precisely because all members of a Craft ritual are expected to participate fully, you cannot be allowed to 'sit in' on one. Nor can a very brief description like this possibly convey the depth of the experience. Ritual works on essential life energy.

Much is written and taught about equipment. Part of a Witch's training is to find and acquire her/his own magical tools (also known as magical weapons). Each tool is both practical and symbolic. For example, the magical Cup represents pleasure, feelings, depth, courage, intuition, Autumn, twilight and Water, as well as its use to hold the Communion drink. The 'ceremonial'school of magic maintains that all equipment must be consecrated and kept apart solely for magical purposes. The more refined and focused each tool is the more sensitive it will be to its task. The 'kitchen' school of magic prefers to keep magical operations centred within everyday life, so the ritual knife comes from the kitchen drawer. This attitude comes in part from the time of the christian persecutions. If a house was searched no special object could betray its owner as a Witch. The custom has persisted as an attitude of down to earth practicality, where the tools are kept firmly secondary to their purpose.

Apart from set pieces of equipment, knife, wand, cup, pentacle etc a Witch needs crafted supplies such as incenses, herbs, and candles. The art of using natural substances to influence states of mind is central to magic. Ideally a Witch makes these by hand. If not the selection is made with care to enhance the work of the rite that is planned. Colours, fragrances and planetary correspondences are combined to aid the deeper levels of the mind to operate.

Ultimately, with training and experience, a Witch can work rituals with no help from equipment or supplies at all. However this is arduous. Imagine trying to run an office for a day without the use of pen, paper, telephone or typewriter. It could be done if necessary, but you would have to be very resourceful, and very experienced in the work of that particular office. Learning to use candles, herbs, incenses etc is done at your own speed. Finding the right time and correspondence with your own feelings is the most important thing of all. A basic ritual kit is simple to put together, and need not be expensive. In due course you may want to acquire more elaborate things which are beautiful or fascinating in themselves. Or you may continue quite contentedly with the very simple things.

15

When you work magic and ritual you may provoke psychic phenomena which are odd, even disconcerting. The strange thing is that normally you'll only realise it's an odd experience after it's over. At the time whatever happens appears quite natural - because it is. It is only our everyday selves that are accustomed to divide the normal from the paranormal that judge things odd. In the Circle between the worlds such distinctions do not apply. However poltergeist noises, thrills and chills are not the point at all, only an occasional side effect. People who want this kind of entertainment would be best off going to the cinema or curling up with a fantasy novel. Film special effects are extremely impressive and great fun, while fantasy novels offer exciting escapes into imaginary worlds. Neither are expensive; both are very available. I enjoy them but do not confuse them with magic, which while it is also exciting and fun is hard work.

Many people are attracted to magic as a short cut to get what they desire. There's nothing wrong with that. Magic is extremely nourishing stuff, in fact, satisfyingly selfish. But you get what you want by working for it. As computer buffs say 'garbage in garbage out'. It's no word play that we 'work' magic. The Craft is not for the lazy, which my favourite story illustrates.

A famous Witch and her new apprentice set out on a journey to a great city. After walking all day, in the evening, they reached a river, broad and shining. On the other bank rose the towers of the city. There was no bridge. They camped for the night.
In the morning the apprentice was extremely puzzled when the Witch set off along the bank heading away from the city. However the young woman's respect for her mentor prevented her from asking questions. During a long hot tiring day she tried to copy the other's rhythmic stride, with some success. Again that night they camped.
The younger woman several times began to speak but the Witch's preoccupation deterred her. During a third day the apprentice trudged after her mistress, increasingly fed up with dust, heat, and a particularly painful blister. At last they reached a ferry, and with great relief both settled on the cushioned seats.
"You've been very patient," said the Witch. "Bathe your face now, and then ask me your questions."
The girl sluiced her face, combed her hair, and began to feel better. "I just don't understand why we had to walk all this way" she said. "All you had to do was a bit of magic, and we could have walked straight across the water to the city. Now we've got to walk all the way back along the other bank."
"Ah, but you see, this is the way to cross a river," replied the Witch, trailing her hand in the cool water.

ThE OLD RELIGIONS

Long before we acquired the Eastern faith of the crucifixion, our ancestors had their own religions here. In sacred groves, by holy springs, among standing stones, the people linked in spirit to strengthen their energy and purpose in life. The great festivals still survive among us, now called Halloween, Christmas, Candlemas, Easter, May Day, Harvest. Together with Midsummer and Lammas these make up the spokes of the Wheel of the Year, times of birth, death and rebirth.

We are learning how sophisticated these ancient peoples, our ancestors, really were. We are learning to be careful of condescending terms like 'primitive' for a society that lacked iron and electricity, yet built Stonehenge, Newgrange, and Carnac.

Not only is a creation like Stonehenge impressive because of the colossal stones transported hundreds of miles; it is also a witness to the mathematics and astronomy of its designers, for the alignments of the huge stones are so attuned to predicting the movements of the moon and stars as to justify the whole being called a computer. The more we face the weaknesses of our own high tech society, the more we realise those 'primitive' societies that still exist often have arts, crafts, medicine, ecology, psychology, morality and social harmony that we lack.

In spiritual matters, most of all, our modern institutions frequently offer us little, and yet we find that 'primitive' people get comfort, strength, joy and meaning from theirs. It's all very well to laugh at odd practices with masks, dancing or spells but if they work, laughter is an ignorant response. Religions descended from the oldest traditions, long before christian times, have been dismissed as 'fertility cults', 'mumbo jumbo', 'nature worship' as if no more need be said. But more does need to be said.

In Palaeolithic art from 30,000 to 10,000 years ago we find the Goddess, the Hunter, the spiral, the circle. The dead are lovingly provided with pots of food and tools for their future needs; scholars agree that this indicates a firm belief in life after death. Scenes of people working ritual have survived, painted brightly on cave walls, that witness groups of people able to coordinate and produce complex ceremony for their needs. The same paintings are full of the animal and plant world, painted with such sympathy and skill for their subjects, that we realise that these people were not separated from their animal and plant kin as we are.

Living in caves suggests to us an uncomfortable, unsophisticated way of life. But a large cave, or complex of caves, offers a warm, spacious home for a clan of families. In fact, a good cave provides a strong, secure structure, better than the majority of buildings, and keeps an even warmth throughout the year. With a river or stream nearby, a number of hearths, and built in rock 'shelving', it resembles today's large house split into flats.

Stone tools sound primitive to us. In fact it takes great skill to understand the types of stone and to flake it to an edge or special shape. Stone knives, axes and hammers measure up well against all but the better types of metal.

But although this is called the 'Stone Age' that is only because it is stone tools that survive the thousands of years for us to find them. Softer materials break up and rot so they disappear much faster. It is probable that there was a pre-stone age culture, with art, spiritual belief, and social cooperation, using only wood, basketry and leather. Some anthropologists now argue a 'carrier bag theory of evolution'. According to this the carrier bag, either woven grasses or leather, was our first tool. Its necessity was for carrying water, food and babies, especially during the summer nomadic months. In winter the bags provided storage in the caves. The theory suggests that it was women who invented this first tool, as women have been everywhere the main water carriers, food gatherers, and baby toters.

Leather and fur can be processed to make soft, warm clothing. Herbal knowledge not only supports health but makes the casseroles tasty too. One modern author believes that a stone age diet is the most healthy and yet delicious. Baskets and pots are crafted with great skill in such societies, providing many of the items we today make in metal.

Evidence from both past and present non-metallic societies is overwhelming that design and decoration enriched all everyday objects as well as special things. This was much more true for them than for us in our mass produced efficiency age. What this wealth of artwork, both abstract shapes and animals, plants and people, tells us is that they cared passionately about beauty, and they had the leisure to create it. Here are two of the essentials of a cultured life. Earlier societies did not divide people into jobs very much so we should not imagine these crafts, or the cave paintings either, as being done by a few specialists. Each family made baskets, pots, clothing; collected fruit, vegetables, roots, nuts and herbs; hunted small game; and made tools of wood and

18

stone. A 'gatherer' way of life was a lot less hardworking than farming, which people only took to when the population grew too fast to live off the land's bounty any more. So everyone had time to develop craft skill.

It is now becoming accepted that the early inventions and discoveries, that are the basis of our history, were all made by women. The use of fire, carrier bags, baskets, leatherwork (tents/ clothes/ shoes), herbal medicine, cooking, domestication of pigs & goats & dogs, wooden tools, gardening for small crops, and pottery form a respectable package of technology. Even the first metalwork, in copper, developed from the use of pottery kilns, and was in the charge of women. Not until after settled communities develop, with the potters wheel, and bronze metallurgy, do men begin to play a large part in our history.

Not only do we find the Goddess images everywhere in early cultures, but everyday society centred on the crafts and leadership of women. This need not provoke fantasies of male slavery, but a kind of mother focused life where older women especially were respected for their guidance. When Europeans met the peoples of North America, who led a traditional way of life, many of the tribes were amazed and saddened that these foreigners ignored the advice of the native women's councils.

It is important to understand that nervous assumptions that female power must have meant male slavery are inaccurate. It is also important not to fall totally into the dream of a matrifocal (women centred) paradise. It was a long period full of social cooperation and secure traditional roles for everyone. Most people had a lot of opportunity to develop the joy of craft skill, and music, dance and song belonged to everyone too. The religion of the Goddess gave profound comfort and meaning, as well as a lot of fun at festivals. Nor was there any war. It's easy to sigh for such a golden age.

However the numbers of people were not enormous, so there was plenty of land for conflict to be solved by one group moving off to live elsewhere. So social structures and religion did not have to handle the pressures of conflict that came later. The lack of war could have been as much due to this as to a superiority of women's government. Also it is too easy to see all peoples of this time as the same. Although the predominant themes were comfortable, cooperative clans, based on women's guidance, and occupied largely by art and craft, with these values expressed in the religion of the Goddess, as in any age there would have been exceptions. These might have been quite unpleasant.

Anyway in general, life expectancy was very different. Some people did live into old age, but many died in childbirth or from disease or injury. We have to adjust our long lived expectations to lives of 20 -35 years being normal. Finally. it was a time of very slow changes, with a kind of hive spirit that would have been frustrating for any restless, independent people; a sort of dream-time when events followed the pattern of the past.

19

I have given quite a lot of attention to all this ancient history. I confess it's partly just because I love this stuff and I can write pages and pages of it. But it's also because this culture I have described is the living origin of Pagan life. We try as far as possible to bring those themes and values into our lives now. Among us, personal crafts are a natural part of the everyday so that few Pagans lack them. The Goddess is central, as is an emphasis on respect for women, and a kinship for animals and plants. Most of all, Pagans have an awareness for former times, and we both honour our ancestors, and call on their support. This means that we are not just a few puny individuals struggling with awful modern problems. We're part of a great flow of descent, the children of mighty ones, who were yet much like us; who successfully worked out the awful problems of their own times.

But this profound awareness of the past is not escapist. I am as happy working my computer to produce this book as I am among the standing stones invoking my ancestors. I think they would have liked the computer too.

'Civilization' is about 8 -10,000 years old. With the arrival of settled life, farming, and towns, we meet Inanna and Dumuzi, Isis and Osiris, Asherah and Baal, the Tuatha de Danaan, Diana, Cernunnos, Hekate, Freya and Odin. Settled life and bigger populations brought stricter laws, more emphasis on men, and about 4,000 years ago, war. Writing, or in some cases a heavily disciplined memory training, led to a college type of learning, and an academic tradition in religion. This eventually comes to us as theology, Magicians and the Occult.

The older cave clan beliefs still survived too, but these enlarged to take in the Harvest Goddess and God, and Goddesses and Gods of technology and civilized arts. These brought adjusted magical practices ('spells') for the needs of householders, traders and warriors. This is what we now call Shamanism. Shamanism survives today, in some form, in almost every society that exists. Well known types are the American Indian traditions, the Voodoo cults, the Bon of Tibet. Anywhere that people use colourful practices to contact a cluster of sacred personalities betrays shamanic survival. So Roman Catholic saints and Hindu gods alike are very shamanic. European shamanism has been named Paganism, from the Latin of Rome. Later, persecution by christianity pushed these Pagan faiths underground. One of the chief of these is what we call Witchcraft.

Witchcraft is therefore essentially a faith of the people, of folk traditions, concerned mainly with the immediate needs of everyday life. It continues the age old faith in female power, in simplicity, intuition, and uses the kind of cheap, resources available to anyone.

But the history of religion we are given is very distorted. Asked what is the religion of the West, most people would answer christianity, even though on reflection they do know that this was an imported mystery cult from the middle east. Asked how long we have been a christian society, many people would say they don't know at all, and of those that have an answer, most would settle on two thousand years because they know the christian calendar divides at that period. Such a long sequence of christian identity appears to make the foreign origin irrelevant. But although christianity started two thousand years ago, like any new religion it took a long time to spread outside its own locality. Even then, a great deal of disagreement remained among the people, who remained faithful to their own cultural traditions.

A small band of christians did come to Britain it seems, during or shortly after the lifetime of Christ, and settled at Avalon/ Glastonbury. They found a complex of religious traditions, only loosely coordinated by a druid caste. These druid priestesses and priests had a system of beliefs not radically different to that of their form of christianity, and therefore welcomed the newcomers hospitably. A church was built at Glastonbury and the Celtic form of christianity blended with the variety of Celtic cults already in existence. People who adopted Celtic christianity did not need to renounce other faiths or practices; the goddesses and gods were not jealous of each other.

Rome invaded Britain not long after. Normally Rome was tolerant of local cults. But the Druids were too successful at uniting the tribes politically with persistent guerilla warfare. As a result, the Romans were uncharacteristically severe on them, killing them in terrible massacres, or persecuting them. Only a few survived to go underground and pass as ordinary people, or to flee to regions outside Roman borders such as Wales, Scotland or Eire. Roman government temples honoured Roman deities, but incorporated local cults in them. So the precious divinities changed appearance a bit and got a new name but essentially stayed recognizable. Temples were sited at older sacred places, and apart from the forbidden Druids' activities, the ordinary people continued to venerate their wells and groves as before. Towards the end of the Roman occupation, the cults of Isis, Mithras and Dionysus arrived to add their philosophies.

But after more than three hundred years of organised rule, the Romans had to withdraw, to consolidate and defend their Italian homeland. Native religion and government took control again. Roman rule never was more than a small colonial elite who built towns and roads with British labour, took British corn and tin in taxes, and left the people otherwise to continue much as they always had. So a revival of Celtic society was an effort, but definitely happened.

Wars against the Saxons and the historical basis of a Celtic central king gave rise to the Arthurian mythos. Much of its stuff came from older Celtic sources such as the Mabinogion. Arthur, Merlin and the Grail has become one of the keys to our national heritage. Recent research is slowly uncovering the culture of this first Britain, and admitting that society survived very well. There is evidence of trading with the Mediterranean cities and the Baltic, bringing beautiful and useful things into the Celtic halls, as well as letters and news. Communities continued at a fair size, with all the professions carrying on their work. Agriculture improved. A better type of horse was bred, and stirrups invented, so that the knight on horseback became a glamorous and formidable force.

Much has been made of the neglect and loss of Roman baths and underfloor heating. However these luxuries were a craze in the last days of Imperial Rome, delightful for the few rich who enjoyed them, but they consumed huge quantities of trees and needed large numbers of slave drudges to tend them. In the Arthurian period people continued to live in the villas as before, but dropped these expensive extras.

The so-called barbaric 'Dark Ages' are much to do with later retelling of the facts from the point of view of church writers who wished to show that conversion to christianity helped savage people become civilized. Celtic religion however did not need improvement, far from it. Celtic faith included reincarnation, a mature code of law which was well respected, all the arts of divination and healing, women's mysteries, a cult of the spiritual warrior, a reverence for art and music, respect for all living things, and a rich store of myth to teach and entertain the people.

Eventually the Saxons settled here permanently, bringing their own versions of deities and magical art. In their turn they resisted the Vikings who then settled in coastal areas, bringing their own fierce warrior cult of Nordic lore. It is from the Saxon culture that we have 'Wicca' from the root WIC 'to bend' interpreted to mean bending reality. Less likely is the interpretation 'Craft of the Wise' but this is still very attractive. Some link has been suggested with the archaic Greek 'oikos' meaning household or community.

At last (but not until about 600 AD) we come to the first christian missionaries as we would recognize them. They were sent by Augustine from Rome. To these monks the Celtic church was horrifyingly Pagan, not to mention the majority of outright Pagans! and they began a determined campaign to bring an awareness of sin, guilt and damnation to the poor deprived people. Unsurprisingly, the people themselves were not keen. It was not until 936 AD that the power struggle ended in the Celtic bishops submitting to the Roman Archbishop of Canterbury.

This is the theoretical beginning of christian rule in our society, about 1,000 years ago.

However, much evidence of healthy Paganism exists after this date. Although the king and aristocracy gave diplomatic observance to the christian church, there were frequent quarrels in this alliance. A famous example of this conflict is the Henry II and Becket tragedy. As for ordinary people, the church was well understood to be a far from a virtuous institution. Chaucer's descriptions of corrupt, hypocritical monks and nuns record how little they commanded respect. There were of course some worthy christian folk, as there always are in any type of community. But the popular judgement of the times was that this was not typical.

The Normans and the Angevin dynasty built many churches and cathedrals. Like the Roman temples, they were usually built on Pagan sacred sites, structured according to Pagan sacred geometry, and incorporated Pagan deities in their carvings and sculptures. This was due to the extraordinary work of the Guild of Masons. They were an extremely powerful 'trade union' whose immunity from christian church control was based on their trade secrets of building techniques; chiefly their knowledge of making a perfect square. They kept their secrets so well that the Church was forced to let them be, and they literally built paganism into the churches and cathedrals they erected. Carved Green Man, Horned God, Sheila na gig peek at us from eaves and cornice as a reminder.

Folk customs of handfasting, processionals, maypole dancing etc continued to flourish. The madonna was allowed to focus the needs of the people for feminine divinity. Much of her image was designed from the attributes of Isis, blue cloak of sky, halo of stars, mourning lady. A plethora of saints and holy days to honour them preserved all manner of other deities. Often the saint's story is the divine myth of a previous deity, retold to fit christian rules.

One of the most persistent deities to survive practically intact was Brighde Brigid, Goddess of poetry, healing and metalwork. After becoming St Brigid, she continued to be venerated much as before, with remarkably similar prayers and customs. Her cult of the eternal flame at Kildare, was not exting-uished by order of the bishops until the thirteenth century. After that her convents continued to preserve her veneration, together with schools for girls and women. One of the greatest was then turned into a women's prison (the Bridewell) in the last century. Brighde customs still survive today among ordinary people in remote communities such as the Hebrides.

By the fourteenth century though, the Church was strong enough to launch its persecutions against heresy. In other words, church authorities were secure and confident enough to torture and kill those whose ideas were different from theirs. Originally the Inquisition was set up to break the power of the Templ-ars, another international order with a lot of Pagan beliefs, whose properties and trade had amassed wealth. Convicted heretics' property automatically became Church property. Later, it was found that when this law was changed, formal charges of heresy and Witchcraft practically disappeared overnight.

Next, the Inquisition attended to the Cathars. These were again wealthy and free-thinking people spread through the highly cultured region of Aquitaine in

23

southern France. Their faith contained much of the same ideas as the Gnostics, early christians of a liberal type. Cathars recognised female priests, reincarnation, and a degree of individualism. They were massacred, and their richly cultured province was plundered by the Church.

Rich, powerful and corrupt, the Inquisition had become an efficient tool for a reign of terror, similar to that of modern Nazism. Once set up, the horrible machine had to apply its skills, or its officers were out of a job. The 'Burning Times' began. The troublesome loyalty of the ordinary people to Paganism had been tolerated long enough. The older social order which had respected women as midwives, healers, visionaries, and local arbitrators had been suppressed, but still partly survived. The Church fathers were embarked on a course of subduing the feminine, the organic, and the pleasurable, which had such momentum that it could only spend itself in extremism. Over three centuries about nine million were horribly tortured and executed. Most of these were women.

Some commentators explain the 'Burning Times' as a kind of group hysteria turned on a minority of scapegoats. Some dismiss the cruelties as no more than typical of cruel and violent times. Some see it as a holy war against an organised grass-roots Paganism which was the religion of the people. Christian apologists claim that the records of their people's brutality are much exaggerated, and it is of course understandable for them to think so. The 'Burning Times' are an embarrassment in the history of a religion of love and peace.

What is definitely true is that both rich and poor suffered, but the poor more so because of their lack of money to bribe their way out. Church technicians in torture were sophisticated wielders of grades of pain. Crushed fingers and toes, wrenched joints, rapes, beatings, broken limbs, were likely to 'persuade' their victims to respond to 'questioning' with the answers desired by their interrogators. Tests such as pricking for witch marks were based on the idea that a Witch must have magical spots on her body that felt no pain. Some areas of the body , such as the back, have nerve endings so far apart as to make natural areas of insensitivity on everyone. Once tested as a Witch, it was inevitable that one would be convicted.

Accounts of such 'investigations' that still exist show clearly how the tortured replied in the style of the torturers wanted. Descriptions of a cold hairy Devil, child murder, and sexual extremes can be understood as the fantasies of the repressed interrogators, getting reflected back their own suggestions. What their victims actually knew of Witch customs is debatable. Some, at least, must have been genuine Witches, but many modern Craft members hold that only a minority of them were. Nonetheless, a widespread caution and fear led to great secrecy and isolation. Even though hardly any executions took place in Britain, beatings, torture, loss of property or possessions, and imprisonment, did.

In such an atmosphere of dread, christianity established its final authority. Covens kept to themselves and set up protective tests for new members to ensure their loyalty. Practices such as desecrating a crucifix may have arisen like this, as a christian spy would have great difficulty in doing such a thing. Witches used only those tools for their work as could merge with everyday objects. Lacking temples, they learnt to cast their circles anywhere secluded. They developed customs such as only recording spells in their own handwriting, so as not to incriminate others if they were arrested and their houses searched. Magical cords were put to tragic use to put a prisoner out of reach of his/her torturers, as were 'Witch's garters'.

By such secrecy and courage the Craft, as it has later become known, survived. But what survived was a fragmented, diminished scattering. In the mid-nineteenth century the people's traditions had become folklore, something continued by some country people with only a remnant of awareness of what they were doing, and of interest to a few scholars.

There is some significance to the fact that most of the supposed Witches tortured and executed were women, but the full understanding of it is not yet in balance. Christianity, together with other aspects of historical cycle, had created a patriarchal society. Women's independence and creativity in government, religion, economic networks and arts had been slowly constricted over a period of three thousand years or so. It appears that the development of a male medical profession arose at the same time as the village Witches were suppressed. Such local healers were herbalists, midwives, counsellors (as well as being as frequently ignorant or con artists as other professionals anywhere). They were largely women and the new brand of male doctor surgeons had law enacted that no one could practice medicine without a licence. The licence only obtained from medical schools that refused entry to women.

The village Witches were few after the persecutions and could not organize effectively against the educated elite of middle class medics. Even though many of the doctors' triumphant 'discoveries' were derived from the herbals of the Witches, such as ergot and digitalis, the village women were discredited to the point that their skill was forgotten. In this century they were remembered only as either simple or wicked, but not wise.

By the end of the last century, Witches had become habitually secretive, and almost extinct except for a few hereditary families. What healing skills, divination techniques, philosophy and ritual remained were distorted and broken by the isolation of Witches from one another. Without the check of comparison and active use the lore became cryptic or partial. Only through determined effort by a small number of enthusiasts has a revival been accomplished.

IN SUMMARY, there have been Pagan traditions with their own wholeness of beliefs and practices, reaching back before the Neolithic, a span of about 10 - 30,000 years. Not until 1,000 years ago was the new christian religion established as the official faith of the nation. Even then it was several centuries before it truly controlled the majority of people's spiritual life, and that only after vicious repression and organised persecution.

We have perhaps been a predominantly christian society for about 250 years.

As the citizens of a new form of society, an industrial, city centred society, we have made ourselves believe that this is superior to the older more country-based way of life. In some ways this is true, for our control of infectious diseases, our speed of travel, building techniques, mechanical communication devices, level of warmth, range of entertainment and variety of diet are all vastly improved. But we are increasingly aware that our medical knowledge is not invincible; our travel, communications and entertainments do not necessarily produce better understanding or social harmony; and insulated buildings, central heating, varied foods and labour saving machines do not balance out against a polluted environment and stressed, under exercised bodies.
The call to remember our roots, and revive our sense of cycle, our attunement to natural energy patterns, and other faculties than intellect or muscle, requires us to look to the older cultures of our ancestors for inspiration and guidance. Many of those in search of answers go to the traditions of other cultures, and through the pre-industrial faiths of Buddhism, Hinduism, Taoism etc find what is needed.

Alternatively, some find it very satisfying to discover a path of equal wisdom right here, grown from the Air, Fire, Water, Earth and Spirit of our own environment.

26

THE REVIVED
TRADITION

At the beginning of this century, the only traces of the Craft appeared to be in children's storybooks, a few odd folk customs, and an occasional scholarly footnote. Yet now, thousands have initiated in the various forms of the tradition. Ritual candles are lit in all kinds of places from bedsits to boardrooms. However, there is no vast underground conspiracy, for the Craft is not one centralized religion, but a loosely connected web of clusters. Perhaps it is because of the recent historical persecutions by those who know what is best for others, that the Craft imposes no rule of orthodoxy in its networks.

Coveners give loyalty and respect to their priestess and priest, but no Witch has authority over another, nor can one coven judge the practices of another. Flexibility and independence arises because the Craft is a revived tradition.

That the Craft survived at all is remarkable. Vehicles such as the Tarot cards and the Qabala preserved Pagan archetypes through the 'Burning Times'. In the last century the Rosicrucians, the revived Order of Freemasonry, and the development of Spiritualism all kept some elements of Pagan wisdom alive. Then the Theosophical movement founded by Helena Blavatsky, did much to establish non-christian philosophy as acceptable in the West. The teachings of reincarnation and karma returned via Theosophical Hindu teachers.

Towards the end of the last century, Charles Leland published "Aradia, the gospel of the Witches". He names as his source a certain Maddalena, a strega (Witch) of Tuscany. At about the same time, the Order of the Golden Dawn was drawing together a nucleus of extraordinary people. With remnants of Masonic and Rosicrucian sources, they began active practice and research into pagan rituals. Israel Regardie, Dion Fortune, W B Yeats, W Butler, Charles Williams, A E Waite and the maverick Aleister Crowley all contributed to the conservation and rebirth of the Western mystical tradition, although these were Magicians rather than Witches.

After the first World War, Margaret Murray and Sir James George Frazer won a degree of respectability by their books for the study of Witchcraft in anthropology. The War had shattered many people's faith in ordinary christianity, and the churches were largely unable to meet the challenge of cynicism and grief. Spiritualism met the needs of a bereaved people and many flocked to the mediums. Many more questioned the religious establishment, and explored new avenues of spirituality.

By the 1940's, an informed social minority existed, involved with pagan myths, alternative healing, ritual and meditation. It must be said that the growing interest in the occult was shared by many top Nazis. This was not at all an interest in the nature faith of Witchcraft, but the unpleasant evidence in this connection does show the loosening of the christian straitjacket.

A retired civil servant, back from the Far East, Gerald Gardner studied Wicca with the Witches of the New Forest. Some of his knowledge came indirectly from George Pickingill, an hereditary Witch who had several active covens in Essex. It is told that it was this coven who raised a colossal cone of power against Hitler's invasion, at great cost to themselves.

When the Witchcraft Act was repealed in 1951 so that Witchcraft was no longer a criminal offence, Gardner published "Witchcraft Today", which openly described Witches' customs and beliefs. The public response to the book was so good that a number of people became seriously involved, took initiation and founded what became known as the Gardnerian movement. Traditional, or hereditary Witches distrusted this movement. They felt that the Craft's survival such as it was had depended on secrecy and transmission through a trusted few. Gardnerians on the other hand, felt that now the law had changed it was time to make the tradition available to those who sincerely wanted it. By the 1960's the numbers of Gardnerians were not large, but well established, in spite of a public prejudice which was still massive.

In the 1960's, Alex and Maxine Sanders began initiating in a more rapid and dynamic manner, catching the enthusiasm of a younger, more radical generation (Alexandrians). Doreen Valiente wrote "Where Witchcraft Lives" and a correspondence and contact organisation was set up by three founder members, using the names Marion Green and QUEST.

The real expansion of the Craft has come in the last fifteen years. People have been drawn to it through various needs. For some there is an attraction to earth mysteries, the science of leys and megaliths etc. For others, it is the healing lore of plants, herbs, trancework. There is the practice of divination which appeals to many. There is the cosmology, ethics and psychology. The fun and depth of ritual, festival and myth is another aspect. Feminists have connected with the Craft as the one surviving tradition which honours the Goddess in primary place. Ecologists and peace workers find in it a spiritual path that deepens their commitment to a world in harmony. Many who have experienced personal growth in modern therapy groups find the source of the techniques and philosophies they already know. Celtic enthusiasts, both academic and intuitive, find much to enrich their existing interest.

The impetus for the growth of the Craft during the last fifteen years has been an increasing confidence in applying and developing the tradition.

While the surviving fragments of Craft teaching have been sincerely respected, they were insufficient as a whole tradition to provide for the needs of its people. Earlier this century, there was a reluctance to develop and improvise, and when this was necessary great effort was made to link the work to older authority. Experiment and adaptation to practical effect has always formed part of a living tradition, as opposed to mere repetition of old forms. But a revived tradition is understandably insecure. For who will venerate and faithfully perform exercises which have been composed and typed up last week? Philosophy and ritual, however carefully drawn from the tradition, needed some genealogy from the past to justify it. So lines of transmission were stressed, and anxieties over authenticity were frequent. If at all possible, an author claimed initiation by an hereditary Witch to back up his/her work, of which some such claims were not well founded.

However, by the 1970's enough experience of using spells, rituals, applying myths and practising divination had amassed for people to feel more sure of their own authority. Some tension still occurs when someone very convinced of their own tried and tested way tries to influence others more than is welcome, but this is not a problem exclusive to the Craft. The trend over all is for the Craft to be understood as a living tradition, re-creating itself in each one of us, rather than a dead structure binding us from the outside.

One of the important functions of any religion is to make us feel part of a continuity coming from the past, through us and into the future. As we share in the same festivals and beliefs as our ancestors, we can transcend the limits of our individual lives, even linking further with future participants in the same thing in the future. In order for such a time circle to take place, we have to be able to feel confident that the rites we enact are indeed held in common with those held in times past, and which we in our turn transmit to times to come. Here lies the very real anxiety about orthodoxy, beneath mere competitive squabbles over who knows best.

But a religion that will not permit its members to be individuals is a source of misery. A religion that will not adapt as a living process to the changed circumstances of each generation cannot endure. For the nature of material world is change. Everything that is part of matter is in flux, beginning, continuing, passing away. A religion too exists in the material world. For each generation new voices interpret old truth so that it can be understood and do its work. These new interpreters often feel they are proclaiming what is actually closer to the original, the older way, than texts and memories decree. But the only other source than text or elders' memory is intuition, the inner authority.

Enquire where the makers of ancient texts, the early lawgivers, where did they derive their wisdom? Eventually you arrive, beyond the most venerable authority, at intuition, mystic insight, the Goddess.

29

Now why, if a text is incomplete, if a line of transmission has been disrupted, if what we have is unclear, why should we not trust our own hotline to the real thing? It may help, it may not, but then written words and preserved memory are not always reliable either. The power of intuition has the advantage that our consciousness is not broadly different from that of our ancestors. We share the same archetypes, patterns, in the structure of our minds. Given an incomplete shape, we are highly likely to select a similar piece to fit the gap as was there before.

In the end, we need to remember that our much loved Craft is not limited to particular words, or sequences of actions. Our rituals, customs, language and myths are vehicles to help us harmonize ourselves with the natural order of the Elements; become more aware of the Goddess and the God, to ultimately go beyond deity to that which cannot be understood. As our ancestors did.

The way we do so is less important than that we do. We find that although the Craft spreads and develops new forms, there is an essence that derives from a traditional core. To me, the Craft is enchanting in its variety. Whoever I meet who practises it, however different their aims and adaptation from mine, there is enough in common between us for me to feel the kinship bond. Having said that with a lump in my throat, I immediately remember that one rarely actually likes all the members of one's family.

Family Tree

The making of a Witch is a personal effort between individual teacher and trainee. It is a tutor relationship, rather than a class one, which allows greater scope for sensitive, intuitive transmission. A particular Witch may be fitted by temperament and practical skills to teach and so become a frequently requested teacher. If this individual teacher also generates high energy by personal magnetism, a large proportion of her/his initiates will in their turn transmit this fiery inspiration onward, and their initiates in turn, and so on. Eventually a cellular network results where a sizeable number of Witches can trace their lines of connection back to the same source.

As there is no international council of the Craft, and connections between the different countries of Europe and states of America form only loose networks, no final authority exists to define what is rightfully Craft. There are no regional committees, and no one set of records to settle an appeal. The tradition exists within its people, a living entity which moves through us to aid us to understand, to survive and to create our lives. Each Witch is given a basic kit of ideas and practice. How she or he applies it is a matter of individuality.

An extraordinarily rich variety results as local conditions and individual need adapts the tradition so that it is reinterpreted endlessly. These different adaptations can appear to have little in common. Many Witches in fact are uncomfortable with the diversity of Craft tradition. Most of us as human beings do feel a deep need for a stable authority to underpin our own efforts to understand things. Few of us are strong enough to feel more than moments of individual sureness, and to be able to claim other authority to back us is a great comfort. The Craft provides little of this, except for the lines of transmission by initiation.

Many Witches express the strain of such spiritual loneliness by criticising other Witches; by condem ing the practice of others as improper, they (we) implicitly claim our own as e real thing. There is a wincing joke current 'not so much Witchcraft, as Bitchcraft' that catches the rawness of the problem. I do believe that beyond and under and within the differences there is a common core.

I have compared what I believe and do with others whose way is very opposite to my own and as we lay out our pieces of stuff, gradually the common inspiration between us becomes apparent. It may be no more than a feeling, a shared attitude, expressed very differently. It may otherwise be more evident in shared practices and our philosophy on a mind level not similar. On the deepest levels I believe there is a dissolving of differences.

Debate renews as to whether a formal structure of membership is necessary. Most of us want to keep the flexibility and independence we now enjoy. For many that was a big part of what drew us to begin with. Some would like to stop the arrogance of self-appointed gurus with their exaggerated claims to 'the real thing'. The existence of naughty ones who ask for money for rituals, charge high prices for spells to relieve infertility/unemployment, or use the glamour of magic to gain media attention or sexual advantage, is a worrying issue. Many would like a recorded membership of a sort similar to a professional association. Offenders who reflected badly on the association could then be 'struck off'. However, although this might prevent some of the abuses, it could also rapidly become a deadening of vital independence.

Codified, booked, laid down, the Craft would lose much of its abundant resource to branch and flower in new and enchanting ways. I care very much about the abuses. But as I believe that each Witch must find their own strength to sort out individual belief, and make their own decisions, so also must every one. Ultimately (sorry about the cliche) we are each responsible for ourselves. A Witch can post prices for magical work to little result unless people choose to pay them. Why people are eager to pay for magic is a key issue about who takes the responsibility for what is going on. As for the occasional use of social glamour as a Witch to gain sexual advantage this is no more than what is commonplace in universities, therapy networks etc. Young women (and boys) need our support to assert their wishes against older authority figures they have been reared to respect and obey. This is not specifically a Craft problem, although the Craft custom of sexual independence can be a helpful influence.

My own chosen method of clearing the abuses is to spread knowledge of Craft practice and principles. When there is a more general awareness that our custom forbids us to take money for ritual work or initiation training, then people will have to face their own motives in wanting to pay. If Witches were openly recognised the media attention on them would have to find more than gosh! wow! Witches still exist! stuff, and the appetite of journalists for drugs and nudity would have to hunt elsewhere for its satisfaction. Insecure males would find it correspondingly difficult to bedazzle younger women into bed if being a Witch was not a titillating secret. The sooner Witches are known for what we are the sooner we can rid ourselves of false glamour and the seekers after it.

The Craft is truly exciting. Its mysteries are as compelling now as they were for our ancestors. Thankfully a growing number of people are becoming Pagan minded and therefore understand. The Craft needs no tinsel. Our Tree grows evergreen in its own splendour.

HEREDITARY WITCHES

Witch families, according to tradition, initiated their children or those who married in. Kin loyalty was the surest keeper of secrecy, and therefore safety. In this century there are some who claim to be the descendants of such families. As such status is extremely prestigious, and extremely difficult to check, false claims do happen.

Generally, as would be expected, hereditary Witches are conservative, keep themselves to themselves, and often express a low opinion of the Witches of the revived traditions.

GARDNERIANS & ALEXANDRIANS

Gerald Gardner's work in the '40's and '50's is the main stem of the modern revived Craft. His 'Witchcraft Today' is a thoughtful book, completely relevant now 35 years after its publication. In a sense all modern Craft Witches are Gardnerian. Those who actually identify as Gardnerians tend to be older, more inclined to a careful, traditional approach, based on Masonic organisation and ritual. They keep secluded in small groups, and hold a deep devotion to Nature. Where possible they prefer to work outdoors. They can now be regarded with respect as the 'old school' of the Craft, pioneers who have succeeded.

From the Gardnerian web come several well known and respected Witches such as Doreen Valiente, Sybil Leek and Lois Bourne. Gardnerian covens are led by a High Priestess and a High Priest.

In the '60's Alex and Maxine Saunders opened out the tradition in a highly energetic and updated way. The contemporary interest in alternate dimensions, eroticism and liberation of all kinds sparked a new interest in magic. The Alexandrian style was very public, using the sensational appetite of the media

33

for nudity and obscure symbols, to gain publicity. Through this exposure large numbers of younger people were initiated; the initiations were frequently based on a very rapid introduction and training. Although many other Witches deplored the mass appeal of the Alexandrian movement, and its theatrical tactics, the result was a far wider awareness of the existence od Witches, and a boost to the numbers who were actively practising.

Many who were initiated through the Alexandrian explosion have long since moved into quite other lifestyles, some completely away from the Craft, and some going much further into a deepened commitment. Alexandrian practice is still comparatively flexible, so that it tends to attract a younger generation. Its customs otherwise are very similar to the Gardnerian.

CELTIC

The oldest origins of myth and custom we have here in Britain are Celtic. Celtic culture comes from Wales, Brittany, Ireland and Scotland. Each of these preserve and develop distinctive variations.

What distinguishes Celtic Craft in particular is a magnificent tradition of art, and the Celtic way attracts many fine modern artists and craft workers. Celtic Witches have their own rites which differ a good deal from the Gardnerian movement. Their tribes (covens) are led by Elders instead of High Priestess and High Priest. Naturally they prefer to draw their inspiration from the goddesses and gods in the Mabinogion and other native sources. Druid traditions and the Ogham script are also key elements of Celtic Craft, but this should not to be confused with the modern Druids themselves.

SAXON/ SEAX

Seax Wicca derives inspiration from the goddesses and gods of the Saxon mythos, and celebrates the eight festivals like other Craft branches. The founder, Raymond Buckland, courageously confronted a Craft tendency to rely heavily on traditional authority as opposed to intuitive and workable methods. He claimed his 'tradition' was all of 30 seconds old! As a result there is now a much more open attitude to what works in practice, balanced against scholarship. Seax Wicca study and invoke the Runes, the Anglo Saxon sacred script.

NORDIC

In common with Seax, Nordic Craft dedicates much attention to the Runes. This is a magical warrior tradition, popular with men. The shamanistic practices of Northern cultures are a focus, as is the nine day sacrifice of the god Odin. The latter leads them to be called Odinists.

Nordic passion for the heroic warrior cultures of the North is stirring stuff. On occasion though some racialist overtones are apparent.

DIANIC

All Witches are Dianics in the sense that they venerate the Goddess Diana. One who calls herself a Dianic however dedicates herself to the Goddess exclusively, and to women's mysteries. All patterns of energy are then understood in Goddess forms. Women's mysteries were a feature of all Pagan societies, but have been increasingly suppressed by modern ones. But Continental Craft always kept a more matrifocal character than the British tradition.

It was Zsuzsanna Budapest, daughter and initiate of Masika Szilagyi, who spread Dianic Craft in its present form. Zsuzsanna emigrated from Hungary in 1956 after the Hungarian Uprising. During the early '70's in Los Angeles she worked in feminist spirituality circles and by the end of the decade her initiates had brought the Dianic way back to Europe, first to France, and then to England.

This is my own original tradition, which I see as an important option for all women. While few would wish to dedicate themselves as Dianics for life, most women need or want recourse to women's mysteries at some time in their lives.

SHAMANIC

Shamanic Craft owes its roots to a variety of sources:- the resources of shamanism, Green politics, feminism, humanistic psychology and the essence of the Craft.

I began as a Dianic, and I still work in coven with women. But the rest of my life as a Witch is now Shamanic.

We use the basic structures and ideas I teach as 'Circlework.' With this simple base for security we follow an intuitive guidance, trusting that what we feel we need to do will always be right. And it is.

Shamanics love chanting, drumming, and simple movement in response to the rhythms. The result is often not beautiful, but deeply cleansing and energising. Sometimes we make really good music, too!

Shamanic Craft is essentially about learning from personal crisis how to heal oneself, and so to heal others, and our world. We try to honour the polarity of light and dark, masculine and feminine, rational and intuitive, above and below equally. This means we often emphasise what we feel to be lacking around us. So we tend to focus more on the Dark, the Descent, the Feminine, the intuitive.

Our leadership is neither a structured hierarchy, nor a collective, but a use of leadership skills in anyone who has them, with strong encouragement for everyone to develop them. We are not secretive; as far as possible we are open with family, friends, employers about being Witches. Our connections with one another go beyond common beliefs or coven loyalties to a lot of ordinary social relationships. It's not so tightly knit as a family, but a squabbling and supportive Clan.

35

There are lots more kinds of Craft around. A lot of Witches share my experience of training in one tradition then later, with growing confidence and self knowledge, creating one's own way according to need. Our 'traditions' are many of them here today gone tomorrow; what matters is an indomitable spirit that survives in yet more new forms.

Shamanic magic is usually very informal
This is Jackie, Suzanne, Geoff, Shan & Tom
weaving a web with a lot of laughter in it.

Opposite: Morgana & Merlin of the House
of Avalon, Milton Keynes. Morgana was born
into the Craft & is now known as Grand
Wicca Mother. She has just recently made an
honest man of her beloved priest, Merlin!

36

37

Priestess.

38

MAGICAL DICTIONARY

A

ADEPT One who has followed a particular path with devotion and discipline for several years or more, and has reached some of its goals.

AIR See ELEMENT/CASTING THE CIRCLE.

ALCHEMY 'The Great Work.' Quest for the Philosopher's Stone which would transform base metal into gold through patient stages of refining. Allegory for the process of refining the soul, or the combining of two into one.

ALEXANDRIAN CRAFT Founded by Alex and Maxine Sanders almost 20 years ago, developing from the GARDNERIAN CRAFT. At first very different because of a much more rapid introduction and livelier, younger style, the tradition has now matured and resembles GARDNERIAN CRAFT quite closely.

ALTAR Table where all the required items for use in a RITUAL are placed ready to hand. Also used as a special place for SACRED symbols, items or images a ritualist particularly cherishes.

AMULET Blend of sacred herbs for protection.

ARADIA Daughter of the GODDESS who came among humanity to teach us the wisdom of magic, in order that we might become free.

ASCETICISM Denial of the natural needs of the body is not part of Craft tradition. Witches understand that the body has her own wisdom which is shared generously with one who cherishes her.

ASTRAL Intermediate state between PHYSICAL and SPIRIT where everyday laws of physics do not apply, so motion over large distances through walls and other objects is possible.

ASTRAL PROJECTION Act of releasing the conscious self from the PHYSICAL body into the ASTRAL, by means of MEDITATION etc.

ASTROLOGY The art and science of DIVINATION by heavenly bodies and their movements.

ATHAME RITUALLY CONSECRATED knife used for INVOCATION. Associations with the East, with beginnings and the power to know.

AUGURY Art and science of any DIVINATORY methods, but principally of OMENS; the foretelling of events.

AURA 'Energy field' of living beings which extends outside the visible body in a range of expressive colours.

AUTUMN EQUINOX 21st September approx. One of the eight SABBATS, or seasonal FESTIVALS of the year. Equal length of day and night between summer and autumn.

B

BANISHING Clearing a place or a person of unwanted influences.

BARD Poetic minstrel caste of CELTIC society whose person was SACRED, as the vehicle of DIVINE language. BARDS trained long and hard to transmit an elaborate library of sagas which preserved history, mysticism, customs and stories. Their favourite instrument of accompaniment was the harp.

BARROW Mound made as part of ancient earthworks.

BELTAINE/ BELTANE/ BELTAIN May 1 May Eve. FESTIVAL of unions. Celebrates passionate energy and HANDFASTING, vows, contracts. One of the SABBATS. The DIVINE union of two aspects of deity. Dance, merriment, leaping of bonfires.

BLESSING Act of CONSECRATING place, object or person. Expression of goodwill directed through the deeper Self to the other.

BLOOD From earliest times recognised as the life stuff; blood flow an immediate crimson signal of danger or death. Yet women bleed as a sign of health and fertility. BLOOD is a powerful way to CONSECRATE, easy for women, by pricked fingers for men. However this is not common to all CRAFT.

BOOK OF SHADOWS Personal book kept by a WITCH to record traditional LORE received through training. Later on this is extended by her/his records of personal work such as RITUAL experiences, SPELLS, recipes, dreams, MEDITATIONS, SYNCHRONISTIC events etc.

BURNING TIMES The christian persecutions of the 17th and 18th centuries when millions of people, mostly women, but not all, were tortured and killed. Probably only a few were real WITCHES but the terrorism of the Church forced the CRAFT underground. The isolation of very small groups that resulted led to the loss of much knowledge, so that by this century only fragments survived.

C

CASTING THE CIRCLE Invocation of safe, energised space within which WITCHES work RITUAL. Each of the four cardinal points (N/S, E/W are INVOKED with their appropriate powers. See ELEMENTS.

CAULDRON

RITUALLY CONSECRATED pot. Symbol
of transformation, for what goes
in it comes out changed. Metaphor for the womb of the GODDESS. Many think
the Celtic CAULDRON of birth, sustenance and death was the original GRAIL.
CELTIA Vigorous, artistic culture which spread over most of Europe about 3
thousand years ago. The Roman Empire then pushed north and the CELTS
became partly Roman subjects, while some kept independence in the wilder
regions. CELTIC CRAFT takes its inspiration from this culture. See BARD,
CAULDRON, DRUID, GROVE **CERNUNNOS** The GOD, HORNED one, oracle.
One of the oldest names for the GOD of the WITCHES. See HERNE.

CHALICE CONSECRATED cup from which
wine or the milk of life, is given. It
is associated with the West, emotions,
intuition, nourishment and the power of
courage.See COMMUNION

CHARGE OF THE GODDESS A poetic passage of great beauty which expresses
CRAFT beliefs. Its true origins in time are unknown. Some parts were contributed by Doreen Valiente as part of the GARDNERIAN revival. Some are much
older, from Leland's' ARADIA the Gospel of the WITCHES' got from Maddalena
of Tuscany at the end of the last century. It may derive from even older sources.
Most modern WITCHES cherish one of its versions, and although it does appear
in different wording each one shares an essential SPIRIT without contradiction.
'CHARGE' is an archaic word for undertaking, or contract.
CHARM Item believed by its bearer to protect and benefit her/him.
CLAIRVOYANT see MEDIUM.
COMMUNION Love feast of thanksgiving which completes the work of a
RITUAL. The CHALICE is passed DEOSIL, and each drinks in turn. Bread is also
passed and shared, together with other food if desired. The pleasure of eating
and drinking together, relaxing and sharing in light hearted style gives a
CRAFT RITUAL an earth root in the power of happiness.
CONE OF POWER VORTEX. Within a CAST CIRCLE WITCHES raise their (life)
energy in order to direct their shared power into a purpose they have chosen.
The shared power of a RITUAL group is always more than just the sum of the
power of its members.

41

CONSECRATE Direction of a deep focus on to an ordinary object, person or place, so that it becomes linked to and saturated by the power of a MAGICAL image. Whatever is CONSECRATED can then remind us, and awaken our deeper minds to the meaning of the magical image.

CORDS MAGICAL tools used especially at INITIATION, and for achieving a desire.

COSMIC Anything on a scale beyond the confines of our own planet. Often used to mean 'SPIRITUAL.'

COVEN Dedicated group of WITCHES who meet regularly to work together. The bond between an established COVEN is more than a working association, a therapy group, or a consciousness raising group. It is more like a SPIRITUAL family. Many WITCHES believe a COVEN may not increase beyond 13. In practice the average number is about 7.

CRAEFTE Power, skill, integrity, craft. From the Saxon.

THE CRAFT Affectionate name given by WITCHES to their faith.

CRONE From the Greek for 'time', a woman who has gone beyond the time cycle of her menstruation, usually after 50 -56 years old. The CRONE is the Wisewoman aspect of the GODDESS, the most feared and least understood by modern society.

CRYSTALS The beautiful gifts of the EARTH ELEMENTAL which, like WATER, take prints from human emotion. Used for DIVINATION and HEALING.

D

DARK Light and DARK = Good and Evil - or do they? Too much light when you want to sleep makes the gentle DARK welcome. The DARK side of life is part of a cycle, an inner night and day. 'To every thing there is a season, and a purpose.' SHAMANIC CRAFT especially honours both DARK and Light equally. From this view to reject the DARK, the hidden, the painful, is as odd as trying to deny the Sun.

DEOSIL Sunwise
or clockwise
For INVOKING
(Scottish
Gaelic)

DEVIL All that is disliked and feared. RELIGIONS such as christianity claim the creative origin of all is wholly 'good', - and yet suffering exists everywhere. Their way out is to identify the source of 'evil' as an opposing god, SATAN.

Projection of all nastiness on to an outside entity allows a believer to avoid responsibility for their own feelings.

DEMON What you fear. See DEVIL.

DIANA Roman MOON GODDESS who inherited elements from Greek Artemis, Cretan Britomartis and Anatolian Hekate. Mistress of women's sanctuary, instinct, freedom, MAGIC, creativity/ fertility, midwife, huntress, she was venerated at Ephesus as late as 400 ad, then later became the Great GODDESS of the WITCHES in medieval Europe

DIANIC CRAFT Feminist Witches who form women's circles to honour the Goddess alone. See WOMEN'S MYSTERIES. Also certain mixed groups who focus on DIANA, usually with an emphasis on female power.

DIVINATION Use of material tools to occupy rational consciousness so that deeper levels of the mind are freed to operate. The intuitive faculty is directed to communicate with other realities, or indicate future trends. (see ASTROLOGY DOWSING GEOMANCY NUMEROLOGY OUIJA PALMISTRY RUNES SCRYING TAROT)

DIVINE = SACRED. Anything associated with the GODDESS/ the GOD/ one's deepest Self. Anything and everything can be perceived as DIVINE at some time.

DOLMEN Ancient stone structure with vertical stones supporting a horizontal one.

DOWSING DIVINATION using a rod or a pendulum to find hidden objects, underground water etc.

DRAG Cross dressing from masculine to feminine style or vice versa. It is not usually an attempt at deception, more a perception game that opens up vision. Especially employed in SHAMANIC traditions to express transition between roles or worlds, the wholeness of the Self.

DRUGS Herbs and funghi are familiar to WITCH lore but there are different attitudes about whether these are acceptable aids to TRANCE and RITUAL.

DRUID PRIEST/ PRIESTESS caste of CELTIC society whose SACRED places were holy springs and GROVES. Their first loyalty is to the Sun, compared to WITCHES whose power is of the MOON. They may have used stone circles as well, but such sites had been created long before. DRUIDS rallied and organised fierce guerilla resistance to Roman invasion. As a result the Romans hunted them down and little of their original wisdom survived.

E

ECSTASY State of intense happiness, unbounded self awareness, joy and energy. Most of us experience ECSTASY through sex, the first stages of being in love, at the peak achievement of effort, or in communion with nature. We can also reach ECSTASY through RITUAL and MEDITATION. It has been described as an 'oceanic feeling' when self and other dissolves into one whole. ECSTASY can be serenity or frenzy, amnesiac, or leave memory of visionary insight.

ELEMENTS AIR FIRE WATER EARTH and SPIRIT corresponding to East South West North and Centre. See CASTING THE CIRCLE, TATTVAS.

EOSTRA March 21 SPRING EQUINOX, one of the SABBATS, or seasonal FESTIVALS. Return of the young GOD, or of the MAIDEN.

EPIPHANY Appearance of the GODDESS or GOD in material form. This can be understood as our experience of the DIVINE in a PHYSICAL event which in itself may be quite ordinary. To a mind trained in the language of MYTH however, ordinary events (the feel of a tree, the visit of an animal) express the extraordinary.

ESBAT COVEN meeting at MOON or monthly intervals, ideally at the full MOON.

ESOTERIC RELIGIOUS or philosophical beliefs meant for an inner circle of people.

EVIL EYE Belief that certain people can harm others by looking at them 'askance' (ie sideways) in a special way.

EVOCATION Raising of malefic power, that is SPIRITS or DEMONS. Risky.

F

FAGGOT In the BURNING TIMES GAY male couples drew christian malevolence, as well as WITCHES and HERETICS. It is said that such a couple were bound together and put as fuel for the fire to burn a WITCH; literally 'FAGGOTS'. This now survives in GAY slang.

FAIRY Small, or human sized personality, whose nature is more MAGICAL than material. They are therefore subject to ASTRAL laws, not PHYSICAL ones. They are different to us but neither inferior nor superior.

FAERY Name often chosen by those male Witches who are especially concerned with their struggle to be a different more creative kind of masculine than the convention today. FAERY COVEN is new in Britain but working well.

FAMILIAR Small animal which chooses a WITCH as a special companion to work with MAGICALLY. Frequently a cat, but can also be a bird, toad, spider, etc. Archaic connections with TOTEMS.

Sapphy.

45

FERTILITY RITES The FESTIVALS of 'primitive people' are often described thus, in a rather condescending way. If we use 'creativity' instead of 'fertility' we gain a wider scope of meaning which makes more sense to our modern minds.

FESTIVAL Special date for gathering and celebration. Through RITUAL including reverence and fun we heighten our energy to an intense focus. The time of year is experienced as a transition in depth. We link to others in a sharing of power as present, past and future participants of the same festival. Festivals set us in our context, self in cosmos. CRAFT seasonal FESTIVALS are mainly SAMHAIN, YULE, IMBOLC, BELTAINE, EOSTRA, MIDSUMMER, LAMMAS and AUTUMN EQUINOX.

FIRE see ELEMENTS, CASTING THE CIRCLE.

FREE WILL We ourselves create what we are.

FUTHARK RUNE alphabet of power.

G

GARDNERIAN CRAFT Founded by Gerald Gardner in the early 50's and the pioneer of the CRAFT revival. Covens have a High Priestess, a High Priest; an emphasis on balancing male and female polarity; follow styles of ritual laid down in the BOOK OF SHADOWS Gardner and Doreen Valiente wrote; generally preserve a disciplined and dignified manner of CRAFT.

GAY Colloquial slang term for homosexual men, and less generally, women. Like WITCHES GAY people have been persecuted by christians, and survived through their own skills of secrecy and courage. Pre- christian PAGAN societies valued GAY people as androgynes who had capacities of both sexes. See DRAG, FAGGOT and SHAMAN.

GEAS Sacred charge of the most serious nature. A person under geas must follow its ban or bidding on pain of death. CELTIC.

GEOMANCY Form of DIVINATION calling upon EARTH SPIRITS.

GNOME EARTH SPIRIT.

GODDESS Origin, creatrix of all, wholeness, everything. Total good and total evil. The sublime and the silly. Intimate friend and cosmic deity. You. Me. Us. Them. Queen of Heaven. MAIDEN, MOTHER, CRONE. Lady of the Ten Thousand Names. See DIANA, ARADIA, KORE, HECATE.

GOD Beloved one of the GODDESS. Her Lover, her agent of power, her Guardian. See HORNED GOD, GREEN MAN, HERNE, CERNUNNOS, ROBIN. He is true masculinity, both savage and tender.

GRAIL Mystic container of desire. Best known from the Arthurian lore, but found as the CAULDRON of Cerridwen in earlier CELTIC myth. Often perceived as a CHALICE.

GREEN MAN GOD of green life, plants, vegetation, forest. He is often found in churches carved in wood, grinning, with vines growing from his mouth. See MASONS

GLYPH Symbol.

GRIMOIRE Magical text written by male academics, often christians, intending to impress each other.

GROVE Several trees close together forming SACRED space. GROVES have been chosen for RITUALS since very ancient times and were especially beloved of the DRUIDS. The sacred Tree has a central place in Western esoteric philosophy; the KABBALISTIC Tree of Life, the World Tree of the Norns where Odin hung in sacrifice, the Tree of Knowledge.

GYPSY Nomadic people of obscure origin, possibly Tuscany, who bore a strong tradition of DIVINATION through TAROT, PALMISTRY etc. Like WITCHES and GAYS, GYPSIES were persecuted by the christians.

H

HANDFASTING Betrothal RITUAL.

HEATHEN Someone who lives outside the town, on the heath. Outsider. (Saxon).

HECATE Queen of the WITCHES, CRONE GODDESS, Dark MOON and Mistress of MAGIC. Originally she was Hek of Egypt, then she was famed in Anatolia (Turkey). Her nature is closely akin to DIANA. She is found where 3 roads meet (Tri-via) the place of decision.

HERETIC A person who chooses their own beliefs and therefore clashes with authority.

HERNE The GOD as HUNTER. See WILD HUNT.

HEX Opposite of BLESS. CRAFT custom has it that to HEX brings threefold of the same result on the sender. Not something to undertake lightly!

HORNED GOD GOD of nature whose origins go far back into the Stone Age. He is animal nature, vigorous and sensitive. The christian DEVIL is a perverted copy derived from christian fear of animal nature.

HUNTER/ HUNTSMAN An aspect of the HORNED GOD, Consort of the GODDESS. A wild, strong, image of male deity. See WILD HUNT.

I

IMBOLC/ OIMELC 2nd February. Festival of Lights. Candles, seeds. hopes, dreams, DIVINATION. British association with Brighde. The time when the first lambs are born and the seeds waken in the dark EARTH.

IMMANENT Existing as matter or some bodily form. The GODDESS and GOD are IMMANENT rather than transcendent. S/he are not above or superior to the PHYSICAL: they are it itself.

INCENSES

Blend of herbs, gums,
spices and resins mixed according
to ESOTERIC ASTROLOGICAL and herbal
correspondences at the appropriate
day hour and phase of the MOON.
Used to INVOKE a desired state of
mind during RITUAL, DIVINATION or
any special occasion.

INITIATION Transition from one state of self to another. As this is both an ending and a beginning the former self is understood to die and the new self to be born. As a RITUAL a WITCH'S personal INITIATION is a coming of age, and an undertaking of devotion to the CRAFT.

INQUISITION Agency of christian terrorism which tortured and killed millions during the BURNING TIMES. Christianity has been responsible for the same cruelty as Stalinism, Nazism and other modern dictatorships. That this affinity is so seldom remarked only indicates how thoroughly christianity itself has controlled historical records and public attitudes. Many WITCHES today are aware from experience that most christians are little more civilised and tolerant than their ancestors were. The BURNING TIMES could easily return.

INVOCATION Calling in from a wide range of a power or faculty, to an intensely charged presence.

K

KARMA Eastern word for the WEB OF WYRD.

KNOTS CORD MAGIC.

KORE MAIDEN, Springtime, new energy. Core of the cycle. When KORE makes her descent to the UNDERWORLD at the AUTUMN EQUINOX she becomes Persephone, Queen of the Dead.

L

LABYRINTH

SPIRAL path which turns back on itself, and spins away from the centre, before it circles in again to reach it. MEDITATION walk and inner quest metaphor.

LAMMAS/ LUGHNASADH 2nd August. Harvest FESTIVAL. The beginning of the harvest season is a time of abundance, sun, crops and vigorous summer bodies. But it's also a time of SACRIFICE as the descent to dark Winter begins.

LEYS Paths of little understood EARTH magnetism, which can be traced in straight lines through various SACRED sites. LEYS appear to cover the surface of the planet. They are believed to belong to the same system of meaning as the MEGALITHS.

LORE Accumulated knowledge inherited from our ancestors. Includes techniques of practical matters, MYTH, MYSTERY, information and intuition of all kinds.

M

MAGIC The Art and Science of changing consciousness according to the Will. (Crowley/ Fortune) Through understanding and using the natural capacities of the mind as fully as we can, we can make changes in our world.

MAGICIAN One who trains in ceremony and MAGIC to achieve power. The way of the magician is more intellectual and structured than the way of the WITCH, whose aim is to feel into natural cycles and work with them. A WITCH works MAGIC as part of her/ his RELIGION but a MAGICIAN more usually does so without a RELIGIOUS commitment.

MAGUS Pompous title for a MAGICIAN.

MALLEUS MALEFICARUM 'Hammer of Witches' written in the 15th century as a torture handbook for INQUISITORS.

MAIDEN A woman who belongs to herself. The young aspect of the GODDESS, energy, courage, playfulness, sexuality, curiosity, intelligence. Necessary state of self -possession before any commitment to relationship, responsibility or children. See KORE.

MASKS
A very old aid
to RITUAL which
helps participants
to move out of
their everyday
identities.
Originally theatre
was a part of RITUAL.

MASONS The Guild of Freemasons was a powerful fraternity in medieval Europe who carefully guarded the secret of building on the square which they derived from the Arabs. As the only builders with the secret they were essential to cathedral and church projects. They travelled in bands from site to site, keeping their own customs, and their christian employers needed them too much to interfere with their freedom unduly. They literally built PAGAN features into the churches and cathedrals! Sculptures, mathematical relationships of measurement and ESOTERIC symbols ensured that much PAGAN lore survived. PAGANS could then attend church and feel at home. In recent times MASONIC RITUALS were a primary source for the revival of CRAFT working. See SHIELA NA GIG, GREEN MAN.

MATRIARCHY See MATRIFOCAL

MATRIFOCAL Centred on the female. This term is preferred nowadays to MATRIARCHY because MATRIARCHY sounds like PATRIARCHY reversed, that is, a rule or dominance of women where men suffer deprivation as a result. There is no evidence that early MATRIFOCAL societies or recent surviving ones cause male deprivation. Rather, that men benefit.

MAZE See LABYRINTH.

MEDITATION Various methods of posture, breathing and mental focus which aim at looping the conscious mind into itself so that deeper levels of mind may open freely to a timeless state of serenity or vision.

MEDIUM CLAIRVOYANT. Person who can open her/ himself to become a channel for another consciousness than their own. Often involved in contact with those who have died.

MEGALITH 'Great stone' used in building the ancient stone monuments which often mark sacred sites. The structures as a whole are also called MEGALITHS.

MENSTRUATION MAGICAL BLOOD, a sign of renewal. A time of truthsaying without and within, so whatever pretences she makes that all is well at other times, the veil is now torn away. Her pain, grief, anger or mere discontent must now show up. However, it is also a time of powerful insight within, excellent for DIVINATION of all kinds. See BLOOD.

METAPHYSICAL Outside the PHYSICAL.

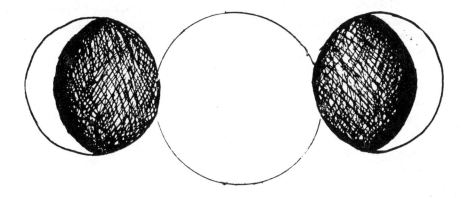

MOON The cycles of the MOON were the origins of measurement, and there are many word links between MOON, mental, mind, mensuration, menstruation, measure. Western MYTH perceives the MOON as female, Mistress of the tides of water, courage and risk, feeling, and all other cycles too. Later christian aversion to an older faith led to a reversal of perception, so that instead of the guide to insight, new clarity and initiation the MOON was associated with madness. The crescents and full MOON are often linked to the Triple GODDESS in her aspects as MAIDEN MOTHER and CRONE. See also DIANA and MOON RITUAL.

MOON RITUAL Adapting a RITUAL to the phase of the MOON enhances its effect. At a waxing or full moon, INVOKE. At a waning or dark moon, BANISH.

MOTHER A woman in mid life who is connected to others. She uses her power for building, in creativity or in children. The mature aspect of the GODDESS, loving, nourishing, involved, angry, fertile, balancing.

MYSTERY Something which can be understood only by direct experience; MYSTERIES can be shown but not explained or taught. For this reason, the core of the CRAFT or any other MYSTERY tradition is OCCULT or hidden, not to deny knowledge to those who want it, but because the deepest meanings are only visible to those who actually look at them.

MYTH A dimension of reality which resembles the everyday - there are people and things in it - but differs because it also contains monsters, DIVINE beings, extraordinary events. It connects everyday matters with the meaning and energy and cycle of SPIRIT through drama, story, poem, song, dance or picture. Its language transmits the stored knowledge of patterns we hold, as a community, through these symbols. See MYSTERY.

N

NECKLACE MAGICAL symbol especially worn by female WITCHES to represent eternal cycle.

NEW AGE We are at the beginning of the Age of Aquarius, interpreted by many as a NEW AGE of SPIRITUALITY, equality, healing and love. Historically this wave of idealistic hope, together with a value on the intuitive skills, occurs towards the end of each century, with an Age of Reason and practicality at the beginning. PAGANS overlap with NEW AGE people but are more aware of cycles that return, and less willing to live predominantly through the mind. See WHITE LIGHT.

NORDIC CRAFT tradition derived from Viking and Germanic sources. See RUNES, SHAMANISM and the GOD Odin.

NUMEROLOGY DIVINATION based on a correspondence of numbers to the letters of your name. Originally a Jewish system. It has links with the concept of mantra.

O

OCCULT Hidden. Not freely available to all.

OGHAM CELTIC SACRED script.

OMEN Natural event which is intuitively received as an indicator of the pattern of a situation. In recent times this has been reinterpreted by Jung and named SYNCHRONICITY.

OUIJA DIVINATION through use of a flat board and a planchet which spells out letters and words when touched. Too often used by untrained persons with uncomfortable results.

P

PAGAN Non christian. From the Latin 'pagana' meaning a person of the country. PAGANS today are people who feel strongly drawn to a SPIRITUAL life based on natural energies, freedom, ecology, pleasure, and the return of the feminine principle. WITCHES are one type of PAGAN.

PAIN The harsh aspect of the GODDESS or GOD. The voice that will repeat its words until it is heard.

PALMISTRY DIVINATION through the lines on the palm of the hand, and the moulding of the hand.

PAN GOD of the Wild. Panic is his cruel but lifesaving gift as the wild self takes over to survive.

PAST LIVES Previous existence as different personalities. These seem to surface in regression TRANCE. Whether these are actual PAST LIVES, ingenious messages from the SUBCONSCIOUS, or ancestral memories, they give genuine guidance which helps us understand our own WEB.

PATHWORKING A narrator guides listeners in a carefully relaxed state through a series of imagined events. The guidance given is an outline, which the listener fills with his/her own images. The aim is to enable the listener to build an inner reality where s/he can communicate with a deeper, intuitive Self. Also known as 'Hermetics'.

PATRIARCHY Rule or dominance by males where females suffer deprivation as a result. See MATRIARCHY, MATRIFOCAL.

PENDULUM DIVINATION through use of small objects in suspension on a fine cord, usually turned wooden spheres, or CRYSTALS.

PENTACLE Metal disc, usually brass or copper, marked with a pentagram. One of the MAGICAL items used to represent EARTH.

PENTAGRAM

Continuous five sided figure forming a star. Symbol of the EARTH, the body, the five senses etc. It has become a favourite symbol of the CRAFT and is part of a formal INVOCATION.

PHYSICAL The dimension of the five senses. Whatever can be seen, felt, heard, touched, tasted or smelt.

PLEASURE Very important principle for CRAFT folk. The GODDESS says 'All acts of love and pleasure are my RITUALS'.

POLTERGEIST A naughty or nasty manifestation in a house noticed as breaking china, moved objects, thrown objects, loud noises etc. with no one touching the things involved. Its source is usually a young person around 13 years old, often completely unaware of their own effects. The great surge of sexual and psychic energy at this age is a rebellious energy, and takes this manner of expression in a fairly strict or repressive family.

POSSESSION A person 'POSSESSED' claims, or is said to have, no real responsibility for what they do while in a state of POSSESSION. Such a person can be understood to have opened themselves to another entity, or to be expressing a deeply hidden aspect of their own self.

PRIEST Male PRIESTESS.

PRIESTESS One who practises RITUAL, so every female WITCH is a priestess during RITUAL. Certain RITUAL work may be reserved by common agreement for a more experienced WITCH. In terms of acting as a channel for the shared power of the group, a PRIESTESS has something in common with the MEDIUM. The two roles PRIESTESS and PRIEST (often called High Priestess and High Priest) express the duality of female and male in nature. Outside RITUAL space a WITCH may become a focus for other people's SPIRITUAL needs; in this sense being a PRIESTESS is less a chosen task than a received one.

PSYCHIC Anything to do with the mind. Often used to describe unusual mental capacities such as telepathy. From Greek 'Psyche' meaning the soul.

PSYCHIC ATTACK A state of depression, anxiety, acute fear, sense of losing control. May involve waking or sleeping VISION indicating the attacker(s) who appear to be using MAGICAL methods of attack. To someone who feels deeply frustrated, hurt and powerless there seems no reasonable explanation for their suffering. An explanation alone would generate more power. Hence the real desperation of facing a more powerful enemy.

Most cases of PSYCHIC ATTACK can be solved if the victim can be encouraged to face their DEMON, to MAGICALLY face the adversary as an equal. Victims of PSYCHIC ATTACK are usually excessively sweet natured folk who don't know how to invoke their own warrior, with healing anger.

PURIFICATION Preparatory stage of RITUAL. A classic PURIFICATION means each Witch rids themselves of anxiety, fear or any hindrance to her/his complete focus on the work in hand through SALT and WATER.

Q

QUABALA Originally a 13th century Jewish philosophy, it was learnt through the mutual protection practised by WITCHES and Jews during persecution by christians. The Western KABBALA now has a distinct identity from its source. Ten worlds, or states of being, make up a MEDITATION system which the practitioner builds within.

R

REINCARNATION The journey of the individual SPIRIT from lifetime to lifetime in order to weave the WEB OF WYRD. Although many people now think these are Eastern ideas they were central to the DRUID colleges, frequent among Romans, and normal to the PAGANS of the so called 'Dark Ages' from Rome's retreat to the triumph of Roman christianity in the Norman period. Until recently we have gratefully used the Eastern word KARMA, but now the custom is growing to use the Saxon WEB OF WYRD. See PAST LIVES.

RELIGION Organised system of beliefs and practices aimed at meeting our needs for meaning in life by providing an approach to the GODDESS, and a code of morality for everyday life. Includes rational, intuitive and mystical wisdom.

RITE OF PASSAGE All RITUAL helps us change and transform our selves. A RITE OF PASSAGE is a RITUAL which supports the kind of change that can only happen once:- physical birth, first menstruation, first sex, first kill, graduation, first child, initiation as a Witch, loss of parents, menopause, clan celebration as elder, death.

RITUAL Series of actions, usually requiring prepared tools, which enables you to clear, then raise and focus your energy towards a specific purpose. Group RITUAL raises energy which is more than the sum total of all those contributing. RITUAL is used to aid any important transition of life; moving house, conceiving a child, having a baby, taking exams, handling money, falling in love, dedicating oneself in love, friendship or business, bereavement, depression or conflict. Good RITUAL is both deeply moving and great fun. RITUALS worked to celebrate the FESTIVALS of the year often develop into good parties after the work is done. But like any other sensitive, complex CRAFT, RITUAL can come to grief without a base of trained knowledge.

ROBES Special robes are worn by some Witches when they work RITUAL. They are a great help in moving from an everyday state of mind to a different one. Anyone who wears a working uniform knows how this feels. Robes also offer men a creative option of colour and dignity which conventional clothing in our society does not.

ROBIN ROBIN Goodfellow, ROBIN Hood are GREEN MAN myths which survived as folk legends.

RUNES

SACRED script derived from NORDIC tradition, associated with the GOD Odin. See FUTHARK.

S

SABBAT One of the eight FESTIVALS of the Wheel of the Seasons. The two Solstices and the two Equinoxes are known as the quarter days. SAMHAIN, IMBOLC, BELTAINE and LAMMAS are known as the cross quarter days.

SACRED Precious and cherished because of its particularly close association with the GODDESS or GOD. Can be anything at all, for everything is actually equally SACRED; but each individual is drawn to particular things which feel SACRED to her or him.

SACRIFICE A deep instinct prompts us to offer what we hold most dear to liberate us at times of great danger or suffering. Older societies were less ashamed of our primitive aspects such as this, and gave them formal expression. Whether or not we accept this aspect of SACRIFICE we must accept that every choice inevitably imposes SACRIFICE of what we are not choosing.

SALAMANDER FIRE SPIRIT.

SALT Creature of EARTH, yet with a strong affinity with WATER. One of the oldest PURIFIERS.

SAMHAIN 31st October. CELTIC New Year. Influences undesirable from the old year are BANISHED. Between the years the veil of time, space and law is thinned, so like BELTAINE this is a time when the different dimensions of reality come closer together. So this is especially the time to remember those you have lost through death or distance to INVOKE their nearness or sharing. Desirable patterns for the new year are INVOKED.

SATAN Christian god form.

SCOURGE A soft whip made of CORDS which used rhythmically (and moderately) creates a TRANCE effect. Part of the GARDNERIAN tradition but not typical of the Craft as a whole.

SCRYING DIVINATION using crystal ball, bowl of inked water, or mirror.

SERPENT/SNAKE Keeper of EARTH wisdom.

SHAMAN Northern cultures' name for PRIESTESS or PRIEST. SHAMANIC people experience the world as alive, all of it, human, animal, plant, stone. This implies a profound awareness of ecology.

SHAMANS undergo a form of psychic death and renewed life through critical illness or mystical trance or both. They then often dress in DRAG to express their role as a maker of transitions. From North America, Eastern Europe, Central Asia, Siberia.

SHAMANIC CRAFT Vigorous tradition of the '80s combining Green politics, feminism, humanistic psychology, rythmic arts of chanting/ drumming/ dance, trancework and radical SHAMANIC ethics with the CRAFT tradition.

SHEILA NA GIG Female figure often found in old churches who displays her vagina for us to venerate as the gateway of life energy. See MASONS.

SHRINE Small CONSECRATED place.

SIGIL MAGICAL symbol.

SIN Painful neurosis frequent among christians.

SKY CLAD Naked. CRAFT custom suggests that RITUAL be practiced SKY CLAD to remove the signs of social differences; to reveal ourselves to each other in honesty and trust; and to remind us of our animal nature. Many WITCHES today however feel that, for them, working SKY CLAD creates more barriers than it removes. A sensitive matter to be decided with care according to individual need.

SORCERY MAGICAL work to control events or people. Not the same as CRAFT. In societies which are struggling with enormous social change, from agriculture to technology for example, old reliable patterns of living shatter. Uprooted people feel helpless, desperately need someone to blame who could be controlled. A scapegoat or villain is identified. Either a mob attack or professional services of another sorcerer make people feel they have more control. Compare the BURNING TIMES with West Africa today. See DEMON, DEVIL, POSSESSION, PSYCHIC ATTACK.

SOUL Individual SPIRIT.

SPELL Specific RITUAL. Frequently designed by a WITCH for others to use for themselves. SPELLS for various purposes have been recorded like recipes through the ages. A SPELL is a practical technique, used as an aid to the will.

SPIRAL Circle that does not join itself but continues to make more and more circles. A symbol of cyclic progress which has inspired us from the time of the cave clans. VORTEX, LABYRINTH.

SPIRIT That which undergoes changes and yet is the same. Not PHYSICAL, so not apparent to our senses, although it is expressed in matter. Understandable by intuition not by reason.

SPRING EQUINOX 21st March approximately. Equal length of day or night. See EOSTRA.

STREGA Italian for WITCH.

SUBCONSCIOUS The inner self which is full of powerful desires and fears, enormous energy, healing power, and dreams. Yet we are not aware of it in the everyday self, at least not without some training in MAGIC or psychology. The UNCONSCIOUS is the non-personal, the ancestors, the world beyond the personal, which is the rest of the UNDERWORLD landscape. From Freud and Jung, modern language for ancient wisdom. See DEMON, DEVIL, MYTH, PAST LIVES, POSSESSION, PSYCHIC ATTACK, RITUAL, TRANCE.

SUMMER SOLSTICE 21st June. Sun at greatest power. The longest day.

SYLPH AIR SPIRIT.

SYNCHRONICITY Theory that there is not really any random event, and that when a striking coincidence occurs it is a sign in a kind of intuitive language. This name for the theory comes from Jung, but the essential idea is traditionally magical. See AUGURY DIVINATION OMEN WEB WYRD

T

TALISMAN Inscribed parchment or metal with symbols for a desired purpose.

TANTRA Way of RITUAL through the power of the senses. Centred on the immense energy of female sexuality. TANTRA is often therefore feared and misunderstood. However, anyone who has experienced her or his own erotic power knows that this can be the simplest and most natural way of reaching the divine timeless moment.

TAROT DIVINATION through a specially designed pack of cards. The images on the TAROT cards are profound archetypes which can unlock deep levels of the intuitive mind to its own wisdom. Of uncertain origin, TAROT cards have served as a form of code to preserve the tenets of the old RELIGIONS through the christian persecutions.

TATTVAS Hindu symbols for the five ELEMENTS: blue circle for AIR, red triangle for FIRE, silver crescent for WATER, yellow rectangle for EARTH, black egg for SPIRIT.

TEMPLE CONSECRATED space, room or building used for gatherings, creative work and RITUAL. The CRAFT adapted to surviving under persecution by developing ways of creating a TEMPLE anywhere, indoors or out, so that no trace was left afterwards and the place reverted to everyday use. Hopes of creating a CRAFT TEMPLE today seem to contradict its essentially fluid and local character, where every home can be an individual temple in its own way.

THIRTEEN Customarily linked with WITCHES as the number in a COVEN, THIRTEEN is the number of MOONS in a sun cycle or year.

THREEFOLD RETURN CRAFT law which warns that whatever you effect by use of MAGIC will return on you three times over in due course, which is why a true WITCH is extremely unlikely to HEX.

TIDES The ebb and flow movement we experience in the seasons, the MOON, in menstruation, in the ups and downs of ordinary life, the sea etc. MAGIC tries to attune to TIDES and work with the SPIRAL.

TOR Earthwork from pre Roman times in the form of a hill. Known and loved as SACRED sites, the best known of them is Glastonbury TOR.

TOTEM Older societies preserve customs of identifying as a clan group with the nature of a particular animal, plant or stone. It is the TOTEM which gives a common bond to the group, not blood kinship, or place of birth. SHAMANS work towards meeting their TOTEM SPIRIT to ask for teaching.

TRANCE State of relaxation and trust in which the everyday conscious mind sleeps and deeper intuitive levels of the mind have freer scope of expression. Can be a source of guidance and self renewal. Similar in some ways to the state of dreaming, but not the same. REGRESSION TRANCE stimulates complex memories of early life, or apparent past lives.

TREE One of the greatest myth symbols. The roots reach deep into the UNDERWORLD, the trunk is here in the everyday, the branches reach up to

the stars. TREES protect and nourish, yet also bear the dying god or goddess in sacrifice. TREES give us WANDS which travel with us so the unmoving TREE parent can see the world. In exchange the WAND teaches us the slower, deeper wisdom of the TREE. TREES are powerful healers, able to soak up anger, grief and fear from us. SHAMANIC CRAFT have an affectionate TREE cult. The SACRED TREE comes into most cultures' myth.

U

UNCONSCIOUS See SUBCONSCIOUS.
UNDERWORLD The dimensions of reality which lie 'beyond' or 'deeper', 'within' or 'under' the everyday. Various labels attempt to map what we can only partly comprehend with labels such as 'unconscious mind' 'super mind' 'ASTRAL plane' etc. The 'UNDERWORLD' is favoured by workers of the western tradition because it lacks the implication of an isolated personal experience which 'inner world' suggests.
UNDINE Water spirit.

V

VISION A seeing that goes beyond everyday looking, that holds guidance. Can be waking or sleeping.
VORTEX Cone of power, SPIRAL.

W

WAND

Stick or staff CONSECRATED
to RITUAL use. Extends the

arm and hand to focus the
direction of the will.
Symbolically either the spine
or the penis. Associated with
determination, energy, success,
FIRE, and the South. Part of a very old contract between TREES and humanity.

WARLOCK Deceiver. Used by those who know little to mean a male WITCH.

WEAPONS Frequent name for MAGICAL equipment, especially by MAGI-CIANS.

WEB OF WYRD Often just called the WEB this is the delicate weave of connections between each thing and everything else in existence. The WEB has purpose, often hidden from us (fate) but leaves vast spaces for our FREE WILL. We experience the WEB through coincidences, provoking events, repetitive obstacles, dreams, signs, etc that suggest patterns to us that go beyond everyday explanation.

What the East calls KARMA we call the WEB, for each thing we do makes the WEB tremble; the tremors affect the shape of the WEB we find ourselves in later, both in this life and in others. From the Saxon.

WHITE LIGHT Popular NEW AGE image of goodness and well being. Comes originally from Judaeo-christian myth, and before that from Persia in the War of the Light and the DARK. However, the Craft, and especially SHAMANIC CRAFT, sees Light as good and bad depending on the need, and also the DARK. WHITE LIGHT is something of a PAGAN joke, implying someone is too fluffy and unrealistic, addicted to prettiness.

WICCA Saxon root word with meanings of 'to bend' and less reliably 'the wise'. WITCHES therefore explain this name for the CRAFT as meaning 'bend-ing reality', ie MAGIC. From WICCA, another name for a WITCH is a Wiccan.

WICCANING RITUAL to welcome a baby.

WIDDERSHINS

Circle made
against the sun,
anti-clockwise.
(Scottish). Used
for BANISHING. In some CRAFT never used, as it is believed to go against nature.

WILD HUNT The GOD as HUNTER rides the night. Sometimes we are hunting with him, and sometimes we are the hunted.

WINTER SOLSTICE 21st December. The sun at weakest power, the shortest day. YULE.

WITCH A woman or a man who has trained in the use of their own natural powers; an INITIATE of the CRAFT. WITCHES venerate the GODDESS; almost all venerate the GOD as the HORNED one. A WITCH works alone, but some also commit themselves to working in COVEN.

WIZARD Term used by outsiders to name a male WITCH.

WOMEN'S MYSTERIES Colleges of PRIESTESSES, women's shrines, retreats, FESTIVALS and rites have threaded our SPIRITUAL heritage from the most ancient times. While the majority of women may wish to celebrate or resort to WOMEN'S MYSTERIES for an especially female festival such as IMBOLC, or during a certain period of their lives, only a few dedicate themselves to its service. Recent societies have failed to continue this ancient respect for women. In the CRAFT it is a charge taken by DIANIC Witches.

WYRD Personal fate. The work of this lifetime. Your sacred dream of the most important things you want to achieve. See WEB.

Y

YULE See WINTER SOLSTICE.

Z

ZODIAC Twelve constellations that fall on the imaginary path of the sun known as the Ecliptic.

67

How to become a Witch

At some point you or someone you know may feel that you'd like to become a Witch. Intrigued by ancient lore, fascinated by psychic potential, drawn by dream, philosophy, omen, the applicant begins to seek her/his teacher, and asks for the nearest coven.

S/he may feel very strongly that a considered decision has been made, a profound direction opened up. Therefore someone should provide training and experience; after all any cult is delighted to receive a sincere application from a seeker.

Not Wicca. By all means ask. Haunt the esoteric bookshops. Set up or join a study group. Go to the big festivals. Just don't expect to be given a form to fill out and dates of coven meetings to attend. They don't want you. Tough as it may seem you are not a desirable proposition. A newcomer is hard work.

Tradition has it that the right teacher will arrive in your life when you are ready, but not before. Meanwhile, what you must do is start on your own.

Start a journal about anything magical or mystical in your own experience, however tiny or trivial. Trivia is the forked road of Hecate.

Try talking to trees and see what they seem to answer. Visit the sacred sites of our land. There are stone circles, woodland groves, standing stones and holy wells everywhere.

Try simple ways of meditating:
Air - sit comfortably, try to just notice your breathing for about 10 -15 minutes. It's hard, but the trying is the thing. Notice what kind of thoughts distract you; these are your tasks in life right now.
Fire - gaze into a real fire's heart and let your mind be guided by its glowing heat. Or fix your gaze on the magical flicker of a candle.

62

Water - stare into a big bowl, preferably dark coloured, filled with water. The room is best not too brightly lit. Just let images and feelings fill your mind.
Earth - Barefoot, or just in socks, walk a circle round the room. If your space is limited, walk 4 or 5 steps, turn and walk back, turn again. After one circle (or about 5 returns) slow down, and breathe deep. Relax the body. On the third circle, slow right down so you're hardly moving, still very relaxed.

Watch carefully for patterns in ordinary matters. Whatever repeats in the apparently chance events around you is trying to tell you something. Observe animals and plants; they are good teachers. So is pain, from indigestion to grief.

Which colours make you feel vibrant and alive? Which make you peaceful? Which are best when you feel very sensitive and intuitive? Which make you feel more sexual? more childlike?

Which symbols affect you? Do you like circles more than squares? Why? Do runes and Qabalistic signs attract you? Explore further.
What is your particular way to the Goddess and the God? You could use whatever craft such as writing, sewing, drawing, woodcraft, metalwork, dance, song, massage that you already know, to express and explore how you see and feel about the Goddess and God.

Become familiar with the Charge of the Goddess, think about what it means.

Look at Tarot packs, Runes, Crystals. Or learn a little Astrology. If you feel drawn to one of these, study it further.

Take your dreams seriously.

Read a few more books. The Craft is not overwhelmingly a way of books and study, so if you're not a great reader it doesn't matter. At least get Starhawk's 'The Spiral Dance' and you'll do fine. If you like reading there's a booklist at the end of this book.

Celebrate the festivals. Again, at the back is a brief introduction to these old Pagan gates. You can do a lot untaught to honour the festivals. Bring autumn leaves and fruits in and decorate your home with them at Kore, the Autumn Equinox, for example, and the same with Spring flowers. Such things are also discreet and do not annoy flatmates, parents or lovers who do not share your interest.

Talk to the Goddess, and the God. You don't need special times or places, and you don't need to sound impressive or terribly humble. They're good mates.

If you're near or in London come to one of our Pagan 'At Home' evenings, on alternate Thursdays. Then there's my 'Circlework' course, which introduces you to Craft ritual and provides you with a small group of people to share attitudes about Pagan matters. It takes about two months and provides the common basis for most of the House of the Goddess clan. It is the first two months of initiation training, although you can do it as a self contained course.

We also have a web of Pagan contacts and other Witches in other parts of the country for if you're too far to visit us, or our style doesn't suit you, or you just want more Pagan friends.

I do not think approaching a group or cult with some wariness is at all silly. Although most of the scary tales in the Press of violence, unwilling sex, and blackmail, are very exaggerated, a few are true. So the first few times you meet new contacts, do so in a public place, or in the home of someone you know. Only go to a meeting in a private place you don't know if you have a companion with you, or you've met these new people a couple of times and feel comfortable with them. This does not just apply to the Craft but to all kinds of new groups and organisations.

What is quite common are teachers who are much more in need of being teachers, to make them feel powerful, than you are in need of them. You have the right to ask any questions you wish, and to get clear answers. Answers that imply the teacher has access to great wisdom s/he can't transmit to you because you're on too low a level of development are just not true. A teacher's job is to learn just how to transmit what they know, which is sometimes difficult, but that's the job. It's not your fault if the teacher can't cope with your question. Watch out for people avoiding your questions. You can ask again if you're not satisfied with the answer. Most Witches have nothing they need to hide so there's no reason not to give honest answers.

On the other hand we do like to keep some of our events private among those we know, trust, and can relax with. This doesn't mean you're not good enough if you're not allowed to come, but it can be hard to relax and enjoy a meeting with newcomers to take care of. The work of magic is also much easier and can go deeper if only experienced people are doing it; sometimes we want to have it like that. So you cannot expect to instantly join in everything.

Also remember that a great many people are still extremely hostile to us, so many of us do keep quiet about what we do, or are downright secretive. However if someone is willing to talk to you at all they should accept your questions.

Don't let anyone be rude to you. And most of all listen to your feelings. They are your finest guides. People can look all right, and there could be nothing you can explain about why you feel uneasy. Trust that. Proceed with care, slowly, checking them out. Or drop them, find another contact that suits you better. Alternatively, people can look very different to your usual crowd, perhaps decidedly odd - some Witches are particularly in love with robes, dramatic hairstyles and makeup etc. But if you begin to feel comfortable with them in spite of appearances, that's what matters.

The bottom line is, the choice is yours. No one can make exploring completely safe or constantly pleasant. But you can always choose whether to go to another meeting or not. And I'm inclined to think that boring, dominating or manipulative teachers are very good teachers! With them we learn not to let people treat us like that in the future. We get that much closer to what we do want.

After doing Circlework, if you continue to feel the Craft is for you, after a while we'll believe you! Then you can initiate.

Initiation takes a year and a day. During that year you will learn more about ritual, and celebrate the eight festivals. You will develop some skill in divination and healing. You will deepen your relationship with the Goddess and the God. You'll begin to see the ordinary as extraordinary, and the extraordinary as normal.

One of the less pleasant aspects of initiation is the claiming of the powers, or the balancing. Whatever sphere of self is the least developed in you, be prepared for that aspect to be tested and strengthened. Are you logical and studious? Dreams and signs and unexpected feelings will flood your reality, until you learn their wisdom. Are you strong willed, an achiever? Events will block you, and take away what you want until you learn patience, vulnerability and deep sensitivity. Are you dreamy, intuitive and passionate? Lists and decisions will press you into clarity and communication. Do you tend to submit or avoid difficult situations? Then you will be pushed and annoyed into healthy anger so you can learn to direct your destiny. It's all about wholeness.

Then you can claim the powers. You can take your place in the universe as an equal citizen where no one can take authority over you. You face the guardians of the five Elemental powers and claim them as your own. You are not a wizard controller of the universe, the master of dread secrets, a superhuman whose will can dominate others. Nor can you telepath, levitate, make thunder.

But you do have a map of your own spirit, a sustaining tradition shared with others, a capacity to enjoy life, and a feeling that if you really have to, you can face anything.

The Goddess

She is most obviously, basic female: breasts, clitoris, vagina, womb, the eggs carried within, moon cycle in blood. Each of us must learn and finally understand the female, whether as women ourselves, or as the other sex, and this is one way to the Goddess. The female creates from her own stuff, building within and then giving birth. What it is to be female, it is that. A woman who chooses not to exercise her capacity to build and birth, must nevertheless live with the structure of her capacity; her femaleness. This is the basic model of creativity. Other dimensions of creativity follow the same shape, and these both woman and man can choose to exercise. Creative power is an invocation, followed by growth, completed by a birth which is also a death, an ending, as the new life is let go. The Goddess is the essence of that, the Creatrix of All.

She is, next, everything. Begin with what you see and otherwise sense by hearing, touching, tasting, smelling and intuiting, around NOW - this book, your body, the surroundings. Extend your awareness through the nearby area, whether building or open space, feel it. Go further to encompass your neighbourhood. Open out to reflect on town, city, county, with all its people, animals, plants and objects. Draw back to observe the whole country full of work, pleasure, pain, conflict and complexity. Consider the continent, the mountains, forests, coasts and plains, the sea around it. Allow the world to display herself, with all the various peoples, the wild places where none live, and the oceans. Spin with the atmosphere, whirl with the planets, go forth to stars, the outer reaches of space, the infinite galaxies. Struggle with the relativity of time, for as one star appears now it has already changed, before human history began. Do not forget the future tense of all that will be! For an instant, before you grin wryly and let it drop, you came near her, because this is another way to her. She is the Queen of Heaven, She who is, was and shall be.

Again, she is the original superstar. Her drama moves the hearts of millions, stories of her rise and fall are endlessly retold. Individuals identify with her to play out her pattern, yet she is never caught for more than a moment. Like the singers, actresses, leaders or thinkers who draw our enthusiasm, she too is larger than life, and unreal. Yet even as we admit her to be unreal she is far more powerfully able to affect our lives than any 'real' person who stands in the queue with us at the supermarket. Archetype we call her in our modern cant, and that she is, a deep laid shape within us all who emerges somehow even where she is not openly recognised. Lady of the Ten Thousand Names she was once called, and that she is, ISIS INANNA, DEMETER, KORE, KUAN YIN, MARY, CERRIDWEN, KALI, FREYA, SEDNA, ERZULIE ...

It is only a few hundred years since last she was openly venerated. In the cults of Mary and Brigid she survived and adapted to her children's needs. Code signals of her passing are 'fertility cult' 'virgin birth' 'dragon/ serpent' 'circles' 'amazon' 'hag/crone' 'three Fates' 'three sisters' 'weaving/ thread' 'oven/ pot/ cauldron' and many more. Much of her lore has been lost, much obscured or retold in masculine terms as the age of the jealous god held sway. Yet even patriarchal science eventually has to acknowledge her. Some top biologists, astronomers and ecologists are now publishing a theory called the Gaia Hypothesis. Logically, they say, the Earth has no reason to have sustained the atmosphere around it with just the right delicate mixture of gases to nourish living beings. This just could not happen as a development of chance. A number of other similarly odd aspects about our planet suggest that it is best understood as a kind of huge organism, which changes its behaviour to adapt to its circumstances. The odd items that provoked notice in the first place are all apparently intended to support living beings' existence. A huge Earth being who purposely produced life out of her vitals? Gaia is the old Greek name for the Earth Mother.

Some people ask if it makes much difference to see the source of life as female rather than male. Isn't the Goddess just God in drag?

We do perceive mothering as very different from fathering; during the last few centuries the difference has been particularly marked. Recent efforts to include men more as birth helpers and so deepen their bonding with their children have led to more fathers sharing the work and the joy of their children and so becoming more intimate, more like mothers. However, this involvement is still centred on the mother - she has no choice about being a birth helper! and breast feeding with all its erotic intimacy is her domain unless she chooses to bottle feed. Later on our deeply entrenched customs and possibly our instincts usually keep a child with the mother if parents separate. And the ancient difference still holds: almost all children know their mothers but a great many know little or nothing of their fathers. The fact that fathering can be such a different thing in different situations, yet mothering is remarkably similar across cultures, history and individual choices, shows the two to be not at all the same.

Mother remains our first security, our first relationship, the first pleasure, the first power, the first pain we receive. Her anger is terrifying, she may not satisfy our needs, yet she rarely totally rejects. She can never deny that we are her children; birth is too big an event. In contrast, fathers can deny us, fathers can leave, fathers can seem to accept us on condition that we are as they wish us to be.

67

Creation myths faithfully reflect the difference. The Goddess gives birth to the universe and her many children within it in the perfectly normal way, with working labour, pain and joy. The gate of life is her cervix and vagina which her images display in sacred art. She is said, later, to rage, to ignore us even, but it always passes; we are never ultimately judged and rejected.

God on the other hand, coming long after to rebel against his Mother and take over, must mimic her vagina with his mouth, breathe, and create by the Word alone. We have been suffering the windy debates of the priests ever since. God then rules in a mixture of love and terror which continually assesses us as we struggle to be good enough. At the end we are probably not, and are ultimately and completely rejected into outer darkness. Insecure in his glory, God is jealous, cannot bear to share our devotion with any other. The Goddess, knowing we are part of her whatever we do, does not mind what name or method brings us close to her.

I realise that this description does not do justice to the more profound dimensions of Judaism, Christianity and Islam. In their more mature forms, and in the efforts of sincere radical reformers, these faiths do offer much the same meaning to life as does the Goddess. Sadly, the more mature forms are less available to most people, so my description deals with the common experience.

As every woman has three stages to her life, so we understand her as our Triple Goddess. Before her first blood she is white, the Maiden. Do not allow the neuroses of the patriarchal mind to mislead you, the Maiden keeps her hymen in whatever state she pleases. She is the state of youth, beginnings, curiosity, the courage to quest. She belongs to herself; that is her true virginity. For modern long lived women the Maiden extends to four seven year quarters. The Maiden is the crescent of the new moon: Artemis, Kore, Arianrhod, Freya, and the young Isis, the young Inanna.

During the fullness of her moon cycles she is red, the Mother. The matrifocal Mother takes on mid-life responsibility, caring and creativity. She is the centre of the outward world. She is organic life, plant and animal, in renewal. She is the all-protective fierce guardian who is yet endlessly tender and always there - that our human mothers cannot possibly be - for they too are daughters. The Mother is the Maker, who creates in pulses of love, pain, anger and satisfaction. She is Leto, Demeter, Nerthus, Frigg, Isis, Hathor, Mami, Brighde.

In her fifth decade a woman passes out of the law of her time cycle, into the dark freedom of the Crone. It is not insignificant that the Crone is the aspect least understood by modern society. Patriarchs need young girls and mothers; they think they do not need the power of the Crone. Anything less like a Dear Old Lady ... she's more of a battleaxe, the ancient Labrys. Fearsome to the patriarchal mind, she haunts us in repressed form as 'stepmother' 'wicked witch' 'the weird' 'Destiny'. Denied her rightful place as council Elder, teacher and adviser, her redoubtable energy turns on itself to our destruction. Given her place however, she is prone to travel, collecting knowledge and having fun; or she will gather in the dark hours to plan changes; her healing aspect, and spirit of upheaval, painful wisdom, and inner transformation interlaces our life systems; her places of retreat are honoured; her work of passing in death is accepted in its cyclic necessity. Dark Moon, Eriskegal, Hecate, Kali, Sekhmet, Hel, the Cailleach, she was called. We must welcome her back among us.

The myths of the Goddess vary, offering us her wisdom which traces meaning in our lives in different ways. Yet essentially the myths are the same. Do not dismiss her drama as fable. Only consider, how like Inanna, the cultured lady of the great city, we too descend into the depths of loss and depression, to hang immobilised in the stranglehold of fear, before in due course, we can rise again renewed. We also know the agony of bereaved Demeter, her anger and despair, and how she neglects the rest of her life because of it. We learn as she did that this cycle too has its return, through acceptance, to a new creation of love. Yet again as the young God grows strong and claims his Bride, then the wheel turns, and even he, the king self, must go down in sacrifice to feed the people's need. Through his giving the son is born of the Mother, and the cycle continued.

Whether we meet the first created one of the Goddess as the Horned God or as Maiden, she is the place where opposites meet. Contradictions dissolve in wholeness. Scholars have marvelled at how death's head Kali is praised as the greatest of beauties; how the savage warrior Freya is also the sweetest of lovers; how compassionate Hathor can thirst for blood. For those who know they are the children of the Goddess, there can be no devil. She is all things to all people, benevolent, cruel, playful, wise, sexual, distant, intimate, silly ... The world was not created good and spoilt by interference. The world was created complicated right from the start, and is as we have made it.

For modern women, the Goddess is an immense empowerment. Once we get past the propaganda about mere (?) fertility and fat earth mothers, we are in a multi-dimensional, feminine universe of power. The Goddess is still fertility, and let us not forget that famine, barren beasts, and the number of children to have are still major concerns to most of the world. For us in a more stable food situation, when to bear a child, and personal creativity, are our relevant fertility issues. Why many of us recoil from the squat round fertility figures of neolithic goddesses, preferring androgyne (boyish) model girls, is a significant question.

But there is far more than fertility to the nature of the Goddess. Centuries of patriarchs have tried to deny female intellect, yet Sophia is Divine Wisdom, Maat is the judge of the soul, Themis is social justice, Arianrhod is detached thought, Tara is the intelligence of the seeking soul.

Modesty and obedience are the proper sphere of the female, insisted the lordlings. Inanna, Ishtar, Isis and their younger sister Mary, are Queen of Heaven, Ruler of the Universe. Aditi is Mother Space, creatrix of all divinities. Cybele demands such dedication to her power that her priests castrated themselves in order to be closer to her. When Nerthus' image was borne through the towns of Gaul no weapon could be left in view anywhere, and all doors were left open in trust. In the groves of Artemis, in the temples of Hathor, Mami, Hecate and Brighde, women's sanctuary was observed by men on pain of death.

Women are so sensitive and gentle, say the masters hopefully, that therefore they must be shut away and protected. But Anat roars with joy as she wades knee deep in her slain. The anger of Demeter blights the earth. Inanna descends as our questing self, a hera of deep courage, to face horror, to die and return. Freya and her Valkyries wheel the battlefields selecting the sturdiest warriors who have died to be their companions. Macha runs swiftly and powerfully to win the race against the best athletes, although she is heavily pregnant.

Woman's place is in the home say, harassed men. Inanna and Isis invented the methods of agriculture and irrigation, and codified the first laws. Athene also is a lawgiver, and the primal Themis. Eileuthyia, Hathor, Hse Wang Mu and many more are midwife healers. Brighde works crafts and technology. Artemis is the excellent huntress of the wild. Bast coordinates the contracts of traders. Women are naturally monogamous, plead guilty men. Aphrodite takes her pleasure as her whim suggests. Maeve conquers more between her thighs than when she rides mighty and valorous to battle. Artemis loves many of her companion maids, though she is said to have her favourites. Lilith left Adam in disgust at his inept attempts in the missionary position, choosing to frolic with Elementals instead. Arianrhod and her maidens disport with mermen on their island beach. The appetites of Freya and Anat are legend.

At a certain age a woman is 'past it', unattractive, fit only to live for the good of others, claim paunchy ageing men. Hecate of the Trivia crossroads cackles at such nonsense. Grandmother Hestia continues to provide her warm hearth, knowing that such idiocy must pass. The Cailleach' cold breath makes such impudent ones tremble. Gaia's earthquakes, floods and tempests demonstrate her undiminished powers. Baba Yaga is indifferent to speculation on her age. Tiamat of the bitter sea is devoured by conflict and yet returns and returns to survive more struggle with the brash young hero.

Only man may be a priest, argue the minions of the jealous Fathergod. Tell that to the veiled Isis, the wealthy caste of naditu priestesses of Sumer, the melissae of Crete, the maenads of Thessaly, the matrons who celebrated Athens' Thesmophoria, the warrior Druidesses of the Celts, the Pagan nuns of Brighde's eternal flame. Tell it to the birds of divination, the Pythoness of Delphi, the

70

millions who burned. Tell it to coven mothers and priestesses today.

For men too these disruptive powers can be immensely liberating. There is no need to be cut off, cramped, into the hard macho mould. There is no need to be solely responsible for the world. There is no need to struggle to control the dangerously aggressive masculinity lurking within. You too are sacred, her child, her lover, her guardian. There are forgotten ways to be male, both strong and gentle, a man of the Goddess - and they are being remembered.

It is not surprising that an exciting, awkward, creative meld is emerging between feminism, ecology and the Craft. Many feminists now invoke the image of 'Witch' to name their claimed woman power. Some go further and train as initiates in the tradition. Old style Pagans have been provoked into a more practical recognition of the feminine principle - not just flowers on the altar, but the washing up too. The Green Movement, Greenham Common and Craft rituals for earth harmony, meet in a common devotion to our mistreated Mother.

With the accoutrements of myth about us, providing us with images of power on every side, we women cannot rely on whingeing that men won't let us... that men are more... that we can't... Because we can. We may risk being disapproved and unpopular but at least they're not burning us now.

Finally the Goddess soars among our dreams, leading us all to strive ever towards our highest ideal. Yet she is earth, organic entity, the biosphere. As the philosophers put it, she is immanent, not transcendant. In common speech, you're touching her right now where your feet touch the floor. She is stuff, matter, things, you. She's not a cosmic judge outside life beyond the everyday. She IS the everyday.

The God

Most Witches emphasise the Goddess as the original matrix of creation, prior to the God. Some Witches however work with Goddess and God energies as completely equal aspects of divinity. Many hold the polarity of female and male energy as the creative tension underlying all life, magic and philosophy. This offers a wholeness not found in other religions which enshrine good/evil, god/devil, light/dark in anxious war.

The God is everything that a male can be. He is provider, protector and guide, not as an appointed authority who remains above and beyond, but as a striving, suffering force who provides by his own sacrifice. He is animal instinct, and as such, playful, sexual, vigorous, at one with nature.

The Horned God is the oldest image of male deity. In northern Europe he is most often shown as a Stag God, but the God with stag horns has been found all over the world. Ancient rites had a man wear antlers, or a stag's head, to represent him. He is the Hunter, who risks his bravery and skill in the wild places. Before the invention of firearms, a hunter was no more than equal to the animal he hunted. Other animals have greater speed, stamina, strength, ferocity, cunning or camouflage than we do, and bow, spear, knife and axe no more than even the odds. A hunter would often return exhausted but empty-handed from the hunt. It was the God who gave success to the hunter - or his prey. He is as much the God of the animals as he is God to us; every creature that runs, crawls, swims or flies is his to protect and decree their fate. We are all animal, we are all part of him.

His names are Cernunnos, which comes from the Celtic, and Herne, which is Saxon. Where the Goddess has clearly marked separate personalities, the God is less diverse, perhaps simpler. His different forms are easily seen as the aspects of the common root that they are. Folklore survivals give us Robin Goodfellow, and playful, mischievous imps, the personification of instincts.

The Horned God as the animal, bestial self, was twisted by the christian patriarchs into the devil they needed to project their guilts. They started with a wholly benevolent deity, so some explanation for natural forces of conflict, pain and wildness was needed. Either these things (seen as bad) are all our fault and dump us in original sin; or some hated agent has disrupted the divine order, so it's all his fault, and we're not responsible. As the Horned One was created by the Great Goddess, so Satan (Old Horny) was created by the christian deity. However, the God of the Witches is nothing like the scapegoat of the christians; he is a vigorous reminder of our true, animal nature, its powers and its responsibilities. He will not allow us to pretend we are more than we are, neither may we sink into disgust. We must accept ourselves, hungry, vulnerable, sexual, competitive, resourceful, selfish, silly, affectionate, determined and wholly real.

To hunt successfully, the hunter must become one with the hunted. To evade capture and death, the hunted must attune to and anticipate the hunter. Each must understand the other's nature, in order to outwit the other. The God is half one, half the other, beast and human. He is the ferocious will, that holds to its goal, and with intuition and practical skill achieves his aim. He is the quickness and craftiness of the beast, whose instinct evades the enemy and survives. Legends of the Wild Hunt, where a human sometimes joins the midnight Hunt, and sometimes becomes its object, reveal the divine law; as you do, so shall you receive in turn.

As the Green Man, the God is gentler, the essence of all growing things, plants and crops. Wild, he grins at us with twining foliage emerging from his mouth. Cultivated, he is welcomed in Spring and cut down in Summer, the Corn King. He grows strong as the Son/Sun reigns in splendour, then gives his body to death so that we may feed. Here is the balance to male pride, to wield strength and ride high, providing there is readiness to give all to the needs of the people. The God is a liberating energy for us today, troubled as we are by the problems of masculinity. The God gives men a model of themselves which invokes love and honour for the female, gentleness, harmony, usefulness. Yet the God is no weakling; he does not suppress his vigour. He is fierce, earthy, determined, disruptive. Listen to instinct, he reminds us over and over again. Be yourself. Listen to women, honour their opinions, learn from them, as the Goddess made flesh they are. But ultimately, your own God-Self is your final judge.

As God of the Winds, Sky God, Cernunnos is the source of intuition, teacher by divination. Messages from the God-Self open up all aspects of male nature, so that not only achievement, but acceptance, are possible. The way of the warrior is endlessly patient practice, brief episodes of heroism, followed by passages of immobility and healing, and overall the protection of small creatures and children.

Odin submitted to the ancient sacrifice of the Shamans to win wisdom. He hung nine days on the Tree; passive, suffering; and so gained more than he could have by force of arms.

The God is awesome power, close friend, and inner guide. For women, he is our hope of sharing the world with men without each destroying the other. Any woman worth her salt comes, sometime, to hate the threat to her that males can be. By all the wife battering, child abuse, rape by violence or persuasion, sadistic pornography, bullying, almost all murders, flashing, street threat and domestic tyranny, we know them as they can be, a colossal system of blocks on our creativity. As responsible, serious females we are sometimes driven to consider ridding the world of them, and so solving most of the problems of violence that exist. If this were all, we should have a duty to do so. Yet each of us knows at least one who is more. At our most hating, we are dishonest if we deny the man who is gentle, supportive, protective and fun. For the sake of these we let go of our ultimate fury, and slog on. If some, or a few, can be real men, then in the end all could be. The God is a way to it.

It can be oddly easy to notice the males we don't like while overlooking the others. It seems to be because it is just those qualities of bravado, bullying or demanding cringer that we detest which are more obvious. The 'real Pagan man' is quieter. Does that mean we want men to shrink back and shut up?

Not really. The men who are particularly valued in our Clan are sometimes noisy, very involved and active, sometimes pushy. Our best wisdom on it is that they are men who don't feel they ought to be in the forefront, don't feel compelled to know the answer to a problem, don't always rise to the occasion. I can think of lots of times the men have stayed quiet when I'm asking for help or resources. Most of the men have at some point announced they need to withdraw from Clan responsibilities for a while - women typically don't announce it so obviously because they aren't struggling with the same press- ure within.

The consequences of a man taking care not to automatically take on responsi- bility, tasks or decisions is that he stays safely within his capacity to cope. So he doesn't get panicked, and stays calmer and much nicer to sit next to.

The more conventional masculine creature keeps leaping into action to satisfy his inbuilt conditioning to 'be a man.' The consequences are that he overloads, panics - probably can't realise or admit the panic because of yet more living up to 'being a man' - and takes one of two paths. The first is bullying and bravado, boasting, dominating behaviour so he can prove he's strong and coping. The second is a sudden breaking into enormously demanding childish behaviour, insisting on attention and mothering because it's tough out there. This is the disarming glimpse of vulnerability which is hard to resist. A man trapped in overload can shoot between these two desperate roles at dizzying speed - the tough guy who's just a baby inside.

What you need to do gentlemen, that's if you're interested in my opinion, (which isn't necessarily so,) is you need to learn to say an inner NO to possibilities for being a decision maker, a fixer, an adviser. This means surviv- ing feelings of not being useful, impressive, or powerful. But you're entitled just to be around without being useful, impressive or obviously powerful. You can just do nothing for a bit. So that when you do come forward you'll not overload yourself into bravado or wimpery.

74

The Charge of the Goddess

The Charge is the nearest thing the Craft accept as a statement of faith common to all. 'Charge' is old English for a contract or vow. The Charge therefore defines the relationship between us and the Goddess.

Parts of it can be found in Leland's 'Aradia: the Gospel of the Witches' first published about 1900. But he got these fragments from Tuscan Witches who had preserved an oral tradition for centuries, at least since medieval times. Their chief name for the Goddess was Diana.

Intriguingly, this region of Italy was once the home of the Etruscans, a particularly strong Goddess people who became an early member of the Roman state. Diana, of course, was then the Romans' name for the Goddess of the Moon, the Lady of the beasts, and the wild champion of freedom. She was especially a women's guardian, midwife, healer, avenger of women's wrongs at the hands of men, keeper of women's sanctuary. Her Crone aspect is Hecate, the most famous Goddess of the Witches.

So it is possible to discern a thread of tradition going back about 2,500 years, bringing us the Charge into the beginning of our own century. Leland's fragments were then lovingly laid out together with other pieces of Craft lore, by Gerald Gardner and Doreen Valiente, in the 50's. Later this Charge was spread by the Alexandrian movement in the '60's and '70's.

Today there are different versions honoured in different places, but all have the same essence. I include here the full Charge (Gardner & Valiente), which is the most widely known, but first I give you the short Dianic Charge. I give you the latter not to promote one type of Craft over others, but because it is much shorter, so it's easy to learn by heart, yet it manages to keep the spirit of the longer one extremely well. When we at House of the Goddess say the Charge together we substitute 'in the heart of each one of us' where it says 'in the heart of woman.'

I would like to honour here
 Robin Morgan whose courage in publicly 'coming out' as a Witch to the women's movement of 1974 brought the Charge into my life;
 Doreen Valiente who I first met in early 1985. Doreen was kind and warmly encouraging to a fledgling priestess who didn't even know that the Charge posters she was enthusiastically distributing were anything to do with this gentle lady in a green cloak.

The Charge of the Goddess

She says,

Whenever ye have need of anything, once in the month, and better it be when the moon is full, then shall ye assemble in some secret place; to these I shall teach things that are yet unknown.

And ye shall be free from all slavery.

Keep pure your highest ideal; strive ever toward it; let nothing stop you or turn you aside.

Mine is the cup of the wine of life, and the cauldron of Cerridwen.

I am the Mother of all living and my love is poured out on the earth.

I am the beauty of the green earth, the white moon among the stars, and the mystery of the waters, and the desire in the heart of woman.

Before my face let thine innermost divine self be enfolded in the raptures of the infinite.

Know the mystery, that if that which thou seekest thou findest not within thee, thou wilt never find it without thee.

For behold, I have been with thee from the beginning and I await thee now.

Blessed be.

Our altar in the Earth quarter of the Temple, House of the Goddess. On the right is incense kit, on the left our Chalice with the Purification bowl below on the floor. Salt is in the round vase on the left of the Earth candle. Branches & pine cones come from outdoor ritual sites.

THE CHARGE OF THE GODDESS

Listen to the words of the Great Mother, who of old was called Artemis, Astarte, Athene, Dione, Melusine, Aphrodite, Cerridwen, Diana, Arianrhod, Isis, Brighde and by many other names. At her altars the youth of the Lacedaemon in Sparta made due sacrifice.

Whenever ye have need of anything, once in the month, and better it be when the moon is full, then shall ye assemble in some secret place and adore the spirit of me who am Queen of all Witches. There shall ye assemble, ye who are fane to learn all sorcery yet have not won its deepest secrets; to these will I teach things that are as yet unknown.
And ye shall be free from slavery; and as a sign that ye be really free, ye shall be naked in your rites; and ye shall dance, sing, feast, make music and love all in my praise. For mine is the ecstasy of the spirit, and mine also is joy on earth, for my law is love unto all beings.

Keep pure your highest ideal; strive ever towards it, let naught stop you or turn you aside; for mine is the secret door which opens upon the door of youth, and mine is the cup of the wine of life, and the cauldron of Cerridwen, which is the holy Grail of immortality.

I am the gracious Goddess, who gives the gift of joy unto the heart of man. Upon earth, I give the knowledge of the spirit eternal; and beyond death, I give peace and freedom, and reunion with those who have gone before.
Nor do I demand sacrifice; for behold, I am the Mother of all living and my love is poured out upon the earth.

Hear ye the words of the Star Goddess; she in the dust of whose feet are the hosts of heaven, whose body encircles the universe.

I am the beauty of the green earth, and the white moon among the stars, and the mystery of the waters, and the desire of the heart of man.

Call into thy soul; arise, and come unto me; for I am the soul of nature who gives life to the universe. From me all things proceed and unto me all things must return and before my face, beloved of Gods and of men, let thine innermost divine self be enfolded in the raptures of the infinite.

Let my worship be within the heart that rejoices; behold, all acts of love and pleasure are my rituals. And therefore let there be beauty and strength, power and compassion, honour and humility, mirth and reverence within thee.

And thou who thinkest to seek from me know thy seeking and yearning shall avail thee not, unless thou knowest the mystery; that if that which thou seekest thou findest not within thee, thou wilt never find it without thee. For behold, I have been with thee from the beginning; and I am that which is attained at the end of desire.

Blessed be.

The wheel

The eight Festivals of the Year are like the spokes of a great Wheel that spins on and on repeating its cycle.

The seasons are a continual process which we must accept and adjust to in our everyday lives.

A lot of magic is about the First Circle, the Circle of Desire, where you learn to assert your Will in your own World. 'Ye shall be free of all slavery' (the Charge.) Yet however powerful we become as individuals there are certain forces that remain beyond our bending, and the seasonal Wheel is the most obvious. For although we can warm ourselves with thicker clothes, heated buildings and transport, heavier food, we cannot be so foolish as to believe we can cancel the power of Winter. Our task in the Second Circle, or the Wheel, is to accept, understand, and work with what we are given as deeply as possible.

Each festival reminds us about the appropriate practical tasks like when best to fix the roof, get out sweaters, make longer journeys, eat lighter or heavier food. It also tells us to let go of the activities of the previous season, so as to really enjoy this one. Finally the Festivals are rich in myth which teaches us about our inner journey as a person. With Goddess and God we can remember the great archetypes of beginning, growing, loving, creative success, struggle, loss, ending and renewal.

Witches usually celebrate all eight of these Sabbats. Our interpretation of them varies a lot from one tradition to another, from one coven to another, from one Witch to another! But by now you'll be familiar with our chaotic manners. The classic interpretations are carefully described in 'Eight Sabbats for Witches' by Stewart & Janet Farrar. I give you here some quick introductory notes which come from House of the Goddess; there's more in my 'Circlework', plus help with how to celebrate a Festival alone or with friends. Alawn Tickhill's 'The Shamanistic Wheel of the Year' comes from Galdraheim coven's experience. His interpretation provides you with a provocative counterbalance to mine because his explores the male more deeply, and he's country to my city.

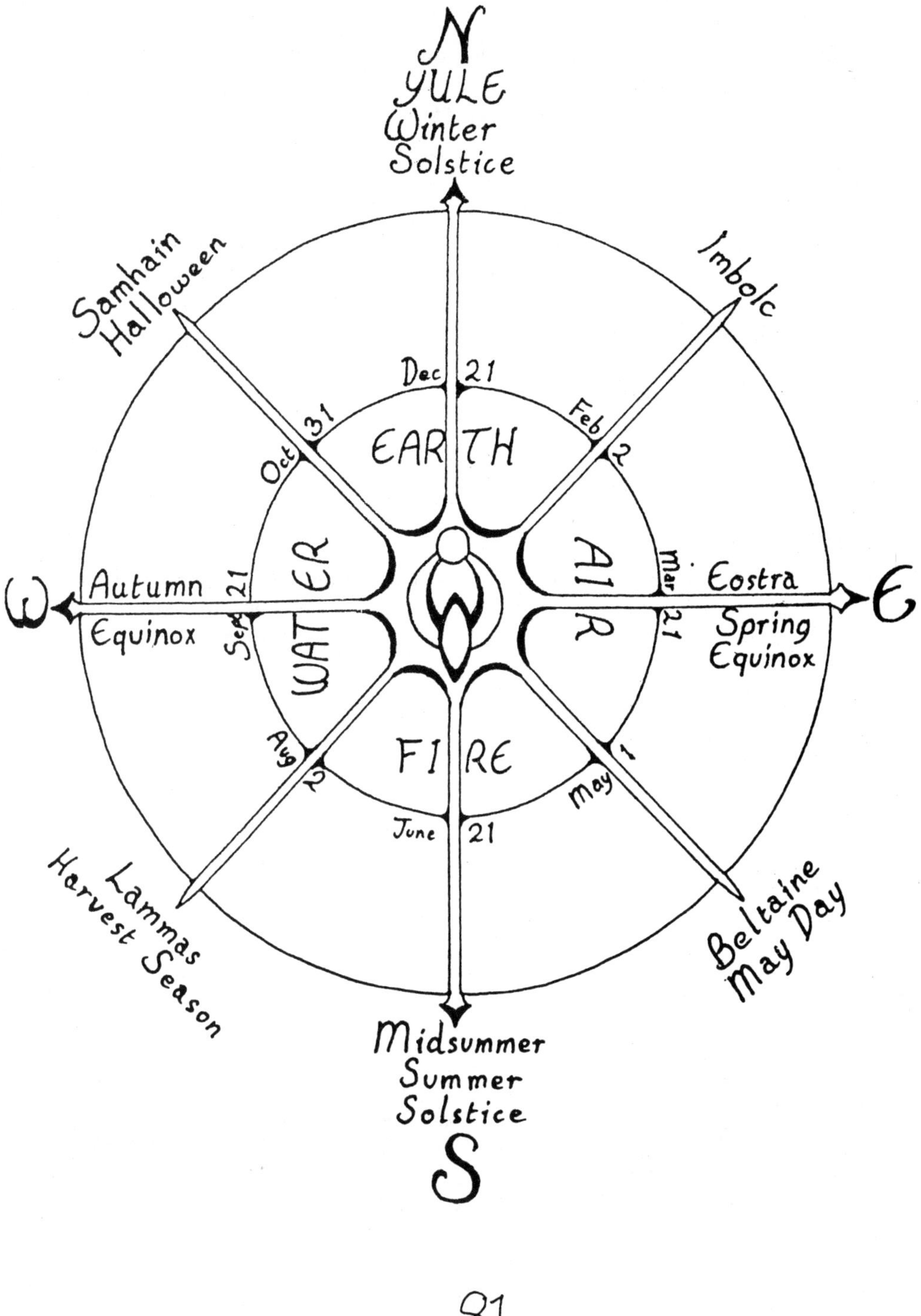

N

YULE
Winter
Solstice

Samhain
Halloween

Imbolc

Dec 21

Oct 31

Feb 2

EARTH

WATER

AIR

Autumn 21
Equinox

Eostra
Spring
Equinox

Sep 21

Mar 21

W

E

Aug 2

FIRE

May 1

June 21

Lammas
Harvest Season

Beltaine
May Day

Midsummer
Summer
Solstice

S

81

SAMHAIN October 31

(Halloween) Celtic New Year. Between the years is between the laws of time itself, between dimensions; an occasion for divination and for honouring your dead. In the sacred drama, the Old God/ the Crone holds the power.

YULE December 21

(Winter Solstice) Sun at lowest. We gather indoors, the earth outside is cool and bare. The sacred son/sun is born, the young god fights and triumphs over the old one, who loses. The mourning Mother comes to our hearth, in need of our cherishing. The sensual body self needs fattening, physical indulgence, and quieter activities from now on.

IMBOLC/ OIMELC February 2

(Candlemas) Festival of little lights. Still dedicated to Brigid, this is the especial festival of the Goddess. It's when seeds awake in the dark earth, dreams and hopes are conceived and spoken.

EOSTRA March 21

(Spring Equinox) Equal night & day. Cleansing wind, enriched air, welcome the return of strength, of Spring, as the young God, or the Maiden. The thinking self makes plans for change and achievement, we eat less, exercise more.

The wheel

BELTAINE May 1
(May Day) Revving up. Testing and sparking. Freedom and liberation. The joy of falling in love, high energy; marriages, vows and contracts, reflect the union of two dancing in cosmic embrace.

MIDSUMMER June 21
(Summer Solstice) Sun at highest. Fire of community power at the beginning of Summer freedom. Processions, outings, dances etc. Night vigil till dawn. Holidays visits and journeys stretch our horizons. The active self comes into full vigour, doing, making, moving, celebrating. Sun worship!

LAMMAS/ LUGHNASADH Aug 2
(Harvest Season) Festival of Sacrifice. The Green Man dies to feed us. Amidst the fruits of harvest in summer plenty there is always a reminder of the dark. Vows to ensure harvest.

KORE September 21
(Autumn Equinox) The Descent of the Goddess. Eleusis mourned the loss of the Goddess going down into the Underworld. As autumn begins we purify, retreat, and prepare for the dark and cold. We turn inward to the feeling self, becoming more sensitive emotionally and psychically.

And so back to SAMHAIN.

83

BOOKLIST

WHICH CRAFT? Shan (House of the Goddess) £3.95
Short easy to read but very informative little book. What is a Witch? Magical Power. Ritual. And a very lively and helpful dictionary packed with easy reference on Pagan ideas and practices.

THE SPIRAL DANCE Starhawk (Harper & Row)
The American Witch whose beautiful book has inspired a whole generation. Rituals, Invocations, spells, careful clear explanations. Lyrical but sensible. Can be and usually is read again and again and again.

CIRCLEWORK Shan (House of the Goddess) £4.95
Not just examples of rituals, but step by step instructions on building your own rituals, as you need them. Extra sections on covens, sex magic, skyclad work, Initiation, Festivals.

HISTORY OF WITCHCRAFT Russell (Thames & Hudson)
Origins and development from early Pagan times through the persecutions to now. Illustrated.

DRAWING DOWN THE MOON Margot Adler (Harper & Row)
Witches, Druids, Goddess Worshippers & Other Pagans Today. Mainly USA material but some European. A superb compendium of research, newly enlarged and updated.

THE WITCHES' WAY Janet & Stewart Farrar (
The classic Witches' text, representing the graceful Alexandrian tradition with clarity and integrity. Reliable, detailed accounts, constantly useful for reference.

EIGHT SABBATS FOR WITCHES Janet & Stewart Farrar
Companion volume to 'The Witches' Way' explaining the eight Festivals in principle and in practice. Sensible and helpful reference.

THE WITCHES' GODDESS Janet & Stewart Farrar
A careful and thorough presentation of the richness of Goddess work coming out of the last 20 years. A good index of Goddesses.

THE HORNED GOD John Rowan
An honest contribution about one male's struggle to embody the power of the God in terms of feminist and Pagan pressure to relinquish traditional masculinity.

85

THE GREAT COSMIC MOTHER OF ALL Monica Sjoo & Barbara Mor (Harper & Row)
Expanded and redesigned edition of an early Goddess classic. Packed with Goddess lore, from all over the world. Full of passion and courage from the old matrifocal cultures and lavishly illustrated with Monica's famous art.

DREAMING THE DARK Sex Politics & Magic Starhawk (Harper & Row)
Earth politics, women's spirituality, the return of Goddess consciousness in a weave of myth and practical politics. A visionary and yet well earthed.

MOTHERWIT Diane Mariechild (Airlift)
A gentle guide to spiritual practice from a deeply female consciousness. Invocations and pathworkings for healing.

THE WAY OF THE SHAMAN Michael Harner
Introduction to the vigorous culture of American shamanism by one of its foremost teachers. Practical exercises in trance and drum.

SHAMANISM FOUNDATION OF MAGIC Ward Rutherford
More detail, with useful extensive quotes from authorities like Mircea Eliade so you don't need to wade through them!

THE WAY OF WYRD Brian Bates
Presented as fiction but really a visionary account of the Paganism of 'Dark Age' Britain. Gripping stuff as the christian spy finds it not so easy to condescend.

THE AWAKENING EARTH Peter Russell (Arkana)
The Gaia Hypothesis comes from establishment scientists who tell us the biosphere we inhabit is as a whole, alive, and has purpose. A wealth of supportive argument.

THE GREEN PAPERS John Button (Macmillan)
Organisations, groups, centres, businesses, books and resources of all kinds which 'will help you live a healthier happier and more fulfilling life - and at the same time ensure that you do no unnecessary harm to the environment.'

86

OTHER BOOKS OF INTEREST

AN ABC OF WITCHCRAFT Doreen Valiente
WITCHCRAFT FOR TOMORROW Doreen Valiente
NATURAL MAGIC Doreen Valiente
ARADIA THE GOSPEL OF THE WITCHES Godfrey Leland
THE WITCH CULT OF WESTERN EUROPE Margaret Murray
THE GOLDEN BOUGH Gordon Frazer
WITCHCRAFT TODAY Gerald Gardner
EARTH MYSTERIES Philip Heselton
EARTH RITES Janet & Colin Bord

WOMEN'S MYSTERIES Esther Harding
WHEN GOD WAS A WOMAN/ THE PARADISE PAPERS Merlin Stone
ANCIENT MIRRORS OF WOMANHOOD Merlin Stone
WOMEN OF MYTH & LEGEND Patricia Monaghan
BRIGHDE'S FIRE Sinead Sula Grian
GODDESSES & GODS OF OLD EUROPE Marija Gimbutas
MYSTERY RELIGIONS IN THE ANCIENT WORLD Joscelyn Godwin
CELTIC MYSTERIES John Sharkey
THE DRUIDS MAGICIANS OF THE WEST Ward Rutherford
PAGANISM AND CHRISTIANITY Richard Cavendish

THE COMPLETE BOOK OF THE TAROT Sharman Burke
SEVENTY EIGHT DEGREES OF WISDOM Rachel Pollack (Thorsons)
FUTHARK Thorsson (Thorsons) Runecasting.
THE ASTROLOGER'S HANDBOOK Frances Sakoian/ Louis Acker (Thorsons)
GUIDE TO THE UNDERSTANDING OF SPIRITUAL HEALING Harry Edwards.
CRYSTAL HEALING Edmund Harold
WHOLISTIC HERBAL David Hoffman
MAGICAL HERBALISM Scott Cunningham
THE OTHER MEDICINES Richard Grossman
HOW TO MEDITATE Lawrence LeShan
SPIRITUAL DOWSING Sig Lonegren

If you would like a copy of House of the Goddess' comprehensive list of book suppliers, occult traders, craftspeople, current magazines, newsletters and regional contacts throughout Britain, send us a large SAE.

87

House of

exists to provide
contact, support, learning and celebration
for Witches, Pagans and likeminded folk.

We have PAGAN 'AT HOME' evenings on alternate Thursdays. These offer a touch of ritual magic to introduce you to Pagan ways. If the city is getting you down, come and share chanting like you never heard before, and pass a well filled chalice around a candlelit circle. Laughter, healing and gossip are all part of it. 7.30pm £1.00

CIRCLEWORK course is 6 days of workshops to introduce Craft ritual and custom. Personal creativity and personal power is a central theme. You learn by practical experience in a small group in the temple. Shan is an extremely experienced teacher and Circlework is her own creation.

We have slowly grown a WEB of contacts in and around London. Our Clan now includes many kinds of Witches, Magicians, Shamans, Druids and Pagans. Some form covens or circles, who celebrate the festivals and hold monthly or more frequent meetings. Many stay alone but like to have Pagan friends. Our lists also have some regional contacts outside London.

The PAGAN HALLOWEEN FESTIVAL is our biggest public event of the year. Held during the last weekend of October, there are Witches and Pagans from all over the country, with dancing, music, craftwork stalls, drumouts, talks and workshops, readers, and of course the amazing Witches' Fashion Show.

the Goddess

SHAN is Clan Mother of House of the Goddess. She is the priestess of the temple and always willing to help people create birth, handfasting, house-warming etc rituals. She also conducts funerals. Ritual work such as this is done at no charge.

Shan is a Shamanic Witch who helps those people for whom it is appropriate to achieve initiation as a Witch, either as Shamanic or other kinds of Craft. She is also an experienced humanistic therapist, Tarot reader, tranceworker. This means help (at low cost) for any of life's nasties.

THE MAGICAL TEAHOUSE is here for anyone who likes this book, and their friends. Open 4-11pm Thursday to Sunday. Lots of sorts of tea, and coffee. Home made soups and salads. Stuffed baked potatoes. Cakes and biscuits. Drumout on Saturday evenings. Very friendly easygoing atmosphere. You don't have to wear a pentagram to be welcome!

If you would like full information about all this, plus details of the latest House of the Goddess events, lots of book suppliers, occult traders, craft-workers, contacts and resources, send us a large SAE.

33 Oldridge Rd London SW12 (01 673 6370)

89

Tissy
A respected Elder of the H.O.G. Clan.

90